101 best campsites
for children

2015

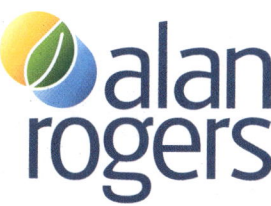

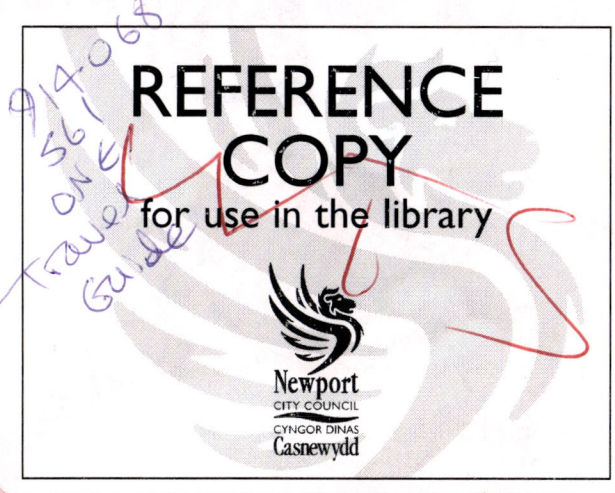

Compiled by: Alan Rogers Travel Ltd

Designed by: Vine Design Ltd

© Alan Rogers Travel Ltd 2014

Published by: Alan Rogers Travel Ltd,
Spelmonden Old Oast, Goudhurst, Kent TN17 1HE
Tel: 01580 214000 www.alanrogers.com

British Library Cataloguing-in-Publication Data:
A catalogue record for this book is
available from the British Library.

ISBN 978-1-909057-59-3

Printed in Great Britain by
Stephens & George Print Group

Contents

Welcome to the Alan Rogers
'101' guides

The Alan Rogers guides have been helping campers and caravanners make informed decisions about their holiday destinations since 1968. Today, whether online or in print, Alan Rogers still provides an independent, impartial view, with detailed reports, on each campsite.

With so much unfiltered, unqualified information freely available, the Alan Rogers perspective is invaluable to make sure you make the right choice for your holiday.

What is the '101' series?

At Alan Rogers, we know that readers have many and diverse interests, hobbies and particular requirements. And we know that our guides, featuring a total of some 3,000 campsites, can provide a bewildering choice from which it can be difficult to produce a shortlist of possible holiday destinations.

The Alan Rogers 101 guides are devised as a means of presenting a realistic, digestible number of great campsites, featured because of their suitability to a given theme.

This book remains first and foremost an authoritative guide to excellent campsites which are ideal for holidays with younger children, typically under the age of 12.

101 Best campsites
for children

Campsite life is made for children. They love the freedom, the space, the ability to run around and explore. And of course there's ample opportunity for getting grubby – and the chances of a bath are slim which is even better news for most under 12s.

For parents there's the deeply comforting notion that seeing your little treasures sleeping deeply at the end of a day in the fresh air is a far better option than seeing them slumped over a techno-gadget in a stuffy bedroom, whether at home or in a soulless hotel.

And of course we all fancy the idea of a child enjoying the 'fun and ice creams' side of the holiday while also learning a little about the big wild world and the forces of nature, meeting flora and fauna close up and personal, interacting with others and perhaps taking on a little social responsibility.

Alan Rogers – in search
of 'the best'

Alan Rogers himself started off with the very specific aim of providing people with the necessary information to allow them to make an informed decision about their holiday destination. Today we still do that with a range of guides that now covers Europe's best campsites in 27 countries. We work with campsites all day, every day. We visit campsites for inspection purposes (or even just for pleasure!). We know campsites 'inside out'.

We know which campsites would suit active families; which are great for get-away-from-it-all couples; we know which campsites are planning super new pool complexes; which campsites offer a fantastic menu in their on-site restaurant; which campsites allow you to launch a small boat from their slipway; which campsites have a decent playing area for kicking a ball around; which campsites have flat, grassy pitches and which have solid hard standings.

All Alan Rogers guides (and our website) are respected for their independent, impartial and honest assessment. The reviews are prose-based, without overuse of indecipherable icons and symbols. Our simple aim is to help guide you to a campsite that best matches your requirements – often quite difficult in today's age of information overload.

What is
the best?

The criteria we use when inspecting and selecting sites are numerous, but the most important by far is the question of good quality. People want different things from their choice of campsite, so campsite 'styles' vary dramatically: from small peaceful campsites in the heart of the countryside, to 'all singing, all dancing' sites in popular seaside resorts.

The size of the site, whether it's part of a chain or privately owned, makes no difference in terms of it being required to meet our exacting standards in respect of its quality and it being 'fit for purpose'. In other words, irrespective of the size of the site, or the number of facilities it offers, we consider and evaluate the welcome, the pitches, the sanitary facilities, the cleanliness, the general maintenance and even the location.

Expert
opinions

We rely on our dedicated team of Site Assessors, all of whom are experienced campers, caravanners or motorcaravanners, to visit and recommend campsites. Each year they travel around Europe inspecting new campsites for Alan Rogers and re-inspecting the existing ones.

When planning

your holiday...

A holiday should always be a relaxing affair, and a campsite-based holiday particularly so. Our aim is for you to find the ideal campsite for your holiday, one that suits your requirements. All Alan Rogers guides provide a wealth of information, including some details supplied by campsite owners themselves, and the following points may help ensure that you plan a successful holiday.

Find out more

An Alan Rogers reference number (eg **FR12345**) is given for each campsite and can be useful for finding more information and pictures online at www.alanrogers.com. Simply enter this number in the 'Campsite Search' field on the Home page.

Campsite descriptions

We aim to convey an idea of its general appearance, 'feel' and features, with details of pitch numbers, electricity, hardstandings etc.

Facilities

We list specific information on the site's facilities and amenities and, where available, the dates when these facilities are open (if not for the whole season). Much of this information is as supplied to us and may be subject to change. Should any particular activity or aspect of the campsite be important to you, it is always worth discussing with the campsite before you travel.

Swimming pools

Opening dates, any charges and levels of supervision are provided where we have been notified. In some countries (notably France) there is a regulation whereby Bermuda-style shorts may not be worn in swimming pools (for health and hygiene reasons). It is worth ensuring that you do take 'proper' swimming trunks with you.

Charges

Those given are the latest provided to us, usually 2014 prices, and should be viewed as a guide only.

Toilet blocks

Unless we comment otherwise, toilet blocks will be equipped with a reasonable number of British style WCs, washbasins and hot showers in cubicles. We also assume that there will be an identified chemical toilet disposal point, and that the campsite will provide water and waste water drainage points and bin areas. If not the case, we comment. We do mention certain features that some readers find important: washbasins in cubicles, facilities for babies, facilities for those with disabilities and motorcaravan service points.

Reservations

Necessary for high season (roughly mid-July to mid-August) in popular holiday areas (i.e. beach resorts). You can reserve many sites via our own Alan Rogers Travel Service or through other tour operators. Remember, many sites are closed all winter and you may struggle to get an answer.

Telephone numbers

All numbers assume that you are phoning from within the country in question. From the UK or Ireland, dial 00, then the country's prefix (e.g. France is 33), then the campsite number given, but dropping the first '0'.

Opening dates

Dates given are those provided to us and can alter before the start of the season. If you intend to visit shortly after a published opening date, or shortly before the closing date, it is wise to check that it will actually be open at the time required. Similarly some sites operate a restricted service during the low season, only opening some of their facilities (e.g. swimming pools) during the main season; where we know about this, and have the relevant dates, we indicate it – again if you are at all doubtful it is wise to check.

Accommodation

Over recent years, more and more campsites have added high quality mobile homes, chalets, lodges, gîtes and more. Where applicable we indicate what is available and you'll find details online.

Special Offers

Some campsites have taken the opportunity to highlight a special offer. This is arranged by them and for clarification please contact the campsite direct.

Calling

all kids

There are thousands of campsites across Europe. Many are fine for children but some really are exceptional. It's not just a question of plonking down a playground or having a couple of small bikes for hire. There should be a willingness to give children that little bit more, a positive rather than a passive attitude towards welcoming youngsters, and the ability to see children as bringing life and soul to the campsite, rather than being a potential nuisance or cause of damage. This guide features a shortlist of just 101 campsites that go out of their way to welcome children and give them the time of their lives.

What's in it
for the kids

Whatever their age, children love camping. They enjoy the fun and novelty of it all; they can make dens, play hide and seek games – and all in a safe environment. There are plenty of other children to play with (having to amuse the kids is not usually a problem when camping!). And of course, being a holiday, there's a good chance of going to bed later than usual.

Much of campsite life is geared towards children, making life more relaxing for all. It's a cliché, but if the kids are happy then mum and dad are too.

Taking it
easy

It's all about families doing what they want, when they want. Take a midday wander around a campsite and you'll find children splashing in the pool, toddlers enjoying the swings before lunch. Some excited jabbering in the distance might herald the arrival of the Kids' Club trooping by on their treasure hunt. Over in the corner, under a shady tree, mum and dad sit in companionable silence, quietly getting stuck into their paperbacks.

For some it's barbecue time; for others it's not long since they were breakfasting in pyjamas. Some, young and old, are getting ready for an afternoon nap, while others are planning a trip to the beach, a pony ride, an ice cream treat… There are choices for everyone and it really doesn't matter, there's no fixed itinerary – this is camping.

Animal
magic

We all know kids love animals. And campsites, with plenty of space and often rural locations, are ideal for being home to farmyard animals such as goats, chickens, ducks, ponies and donkeys.

It is not unknown for the most popular feature on some sites to be the small animal enclosure, not the state of the art pool complex with all its waterslides and water-based excitement.

Activities

for the active

Children want action and there's nowhere better to find it than on a campsite. Many campsites offer a range of activities, from simple home-spun pursuits (think fossil hunting on a Dorset beach or an on-site treasure trail) to impressive sports facilities and supervised activities (perhaps junior quad biking or football coaching).

Activities
galore...

Well equipped campsites might offer any of the following activities: pony riding, cycling, minigolf for the younger ones. For slightly older children there might be tennis, archery and watersports. And that's before you start talking about the impressive aqua parks springing up on many continental campsites, complete with waterslides, lagoons, wave machines and huge waterchutes.

Join
the club

Children love camping, and campsites love children. That's why many campsites run their own children's clubs, often in high season. Most good ones will be multilingual (though language barriers often seem not to exist among children). Clubs may be free, depending on what's on offer and activities may range from organised treasure hunts, group activities like painting, crafts, nature rambles and ball games. Some even arrange kids' talent shows.

That's
entertainment

Many campsites lay on organised entertainment, especially in high season, and often this is free of charge. It might be local music evenings, a family talent show or disco, fancy dress competition or a magic show. Good campsites will ensure appropriate events for different age groups. Of course, such entertainment may not be on your wish list: if so, a useful rule of thumb is that the larger the campsite, the more likely it is that it will offer regular organised entertainment in high season.

Life through
a child's eye

For many, part of the appeal of camping is that it gives a different perspective on the mundane aspects of everyday life. Children generally view this as an adventure, and for younger children just beginning to stretch their wings, a campsite provides a perfect environment (safe, friendly) to enjoy such adventures.

So, whether holidaying in the UK or abroad, the simple task of buying bread from the campsite shop often becomes a fun part of the holiday for the intrepid seven year old. Handing over some coins, saying 'Hello' or 'Bonjour' and returning to base without nibbling too much is often a small milestone in the early years.

Fresh
experiences

When camping, so much is new and unfamiliar. There's always the excitement and anticipation of arriving at your site and choosing your pitch – home for the holiday. Setting up camp, meeting the neighbours and getting organised is always fun. Unpacking all the outdoor games and trying to play everything at once, then clamouring for a swim, or an ice cream… probably both.

The washing up ritual is peculiar to camping. While at home this is no more than routine drudgery of everyday life, on a campsite somehow it can become part of a family bonding team building exercise, enlivened by banter at the sinks with total strangers. Kids seem to love it!

Evenings may be an opportunity to enjoy some organised entertainment: depending on location, this might be Breton bagpipes, a Scottish dancing demonstration, a cheesy song and dance routine or a mock talent show. Unlikely to be highbrow culture but the youngsters generally enjoy the novelty of it all, being outdoors under the stars (hopefully), running around until later than usual.

And when it's time to turn in, the chances are the younger children will be sleepy and ready to drop off. But the notion of sliding into a comfy sleeping bag always seems more fun than just another bed.

Q&A

Do campsites have WiFi?
Many do, usually for a charge.

My children don't speak French/other languages!
Don't worry, language barriers are not so important for the under 12s. Children of all nationalities seem to make friends and happily run around on a campsite.

Are campsite discos suitable for younger children?
Well run campsites will ensure these are age restricted, with sensible and fair end times. Some are for 'all the family' while others are definitely for older teenagers.

How safe are campsites for young children?
Safety is a big issue on all campsites and good campsites will have rules and procedures in place to enforce this. For example, rules may apply to usage of washblocks or the play area. While generally speaking children can run around safely, usual parental responsibilities still apply.

Are babysitting and crèche facilities available?
Some sites do offer babysitting (likely to depend on willing summer staff). Crèche services are less common, though children's clubs run by the campsite tend to fulfil such needs. Of course, these will vary widely.

Do campsites provide baby equipment?
Most campsites can provide a 'baby pack' (cot and highchair) but this is mostly for the accommodation market (e.g. mobile homes).

Enjoy...!

Whether you're an 'old hand' or are contemplating your first trip, a regular reader of our Guides or a new 'convert', we wish you well in your travels and hope we have been able to help in some way. We are, of course, also out and about ourselves, visiting sites, talking to owners and readers, and generally checking on standards and new developments. We hope to bump into you!

Wishing you thoroughly enjoyable camping and caravanning in 2015 – favoured by good weather of course!

The Alan Rogers Team

Facilities
Facilities: The large sanitary block has underfloor heating, some private cabins, plus excellent facilities for babies, children and disabled visitors. Laundry facilities. Motorcaravan services. Fridge box hire. Bar. Restaurant and takeaway with at least one open all year. Pizzeria. Good shop. Playgrounds. Children's activity programme. Child minding (day nursery) in high season. Sports field. Archery. Youth room with games, pool and billiards. TV room with Sky. Open-air cinema. Mountain bike hire. Aquapark (1/5-30/9). Surf bikes and pedaloes. Canoes and mini sailboats for rent. Fishing. Extensive daily entertainment programme (mid May-mid Oct). Dogs are not accepted in high season (July/Aug). WiFi (charged). Off site: Tennis and minigolf nearby. Riding 6 km. Golf 12 km.

Open: All year.

Directions: From Inntal autobahn (A12) take Brenner autobahn (A13) as far as Innsbruck-sud/Natters exit (no. 3). Turn left by Shell petrol station onto B182 to Natters. At roundabout take first exit and immediately right again and follow signs to site 4 km. Do not use sat nav for final approach to site, follow camping signs.

GPS: 47.23755, 11.34201

Charges guide
Per unit incl. 2 persons
and electricity € 24,45 - € 33,25

extra person	€ 6,10 - € 9,00
child (under 13 yrs)	€ 4,80 - € 6,50
dog (excl. July/Aug)	€ 4,50 - € 5,00

Special weekly, winter, summer and Christmas packages.

Ferienparadies Natterer See

Natterer See 1, A-6161 Natters (Tirol)
t: 051 254 6732 e: info@natterersee.com
alanrogers.com/AU0060 www.natterersee.com

Accommodation: ☑ Pitch ◯ Mobile home/chalet ◯ Hotel/B&B ☑ Apartment

In a quiet location arranged around two lakes and set amidst beautiful alpine scenery, this site founded in 1930 is renowned as one of Austria's top sites. Over the last few years many improvements have been carried out and pride of place goes to the innovative, award-winning, multifunctional building at the entrance to the site. This contains all of the sanitary facilities expected of a top site, including a special section for children, private bathrooms to rent and also a dog bath. The reception, shop, café/bar/bistro and cinema are on the ground floor, and on the upper floor is a panoramic lounge. Almost all of the 235 pitches are for tourers. They are terraced, set on gravel/grass, all have electricity and most offer a splendid view of the mountains. The site's lakeside restaurant with bar and large terrace has a good menu and is the ideal place to spend the evening. With a bus every hour and the city centre only 19 minutes away this is also a good site from which to visit Innsbruck. The Innsbruck Card is available at reception and allows free bus transport in the city, including a sightseeing tour, free entry to museums and one cable car trip.

You might like to know
The new sanitary facilities are second to none, with amazing 'thunder and lightning' showers, great fun for children!

- ◯ Multi-lingual children's club – pre-school
- ☑ Multi-lingual children's club – 5-10 year olds
- ☑ Multi-lingual children's club – 10-14 year olds
- ☑ Creative crafts
- ☑ Bicycle hire for children
- ☑ Facilities for children in the wash blocks
- ☑ Children's pool
- ☑ Children's play area
- ☑ Crèche and/or babysitting
- ☑ Local information of interest for children

Facilities: Two outstanding sanitary blocks (heated in cool weather). One includes en-suite toilet/basin/shower rooms, the other also has individual bathrooms to rent. Facilities for disabled visitors in second block. New facilities for children. Baby room. Laundry facilities. Drying rooms. Freezer. Motorcaravan services. Restaurant. Bar. Snack kiosk. Shop. Playground. New indoor play area. Topi club, kindergarten and organised activities for children in high season. Youth room. Fishing. Bicycle hire. Riding. WiFi (charged). Off site: Kramsach 3 km.

Open: All year.

Directions: Take exit 32 for Kramsach from the A12 autobahn and turn right at roundabout, then immediately left following signs for Zu den Seen in village. After 3 km. turn right at site sign. Note: Seeblick Toni is the second site – past Camping Seehof on the left.

GPS: 47.46109, 11.90647

Charges guide

Per unit incl. 2 persons
and electricity € 25,50 - € 38,50

extra person € 5,50 - € 10,00
child (under 14 yrs) € 5,00 - € 6,50
dog € 4,20 - € 5,50

Austria – Kramsach

Camping Seeblick Toni

Reintalersee, Moosen 46, A-6233 Kramsach (Tirol)
t: 053 376 3544 e: info@camping-seeblick.at
alanrogers.com/AU0100 www.camping-seeblick.at

Accommodation: ⊘ Pitch ⊘ Mobile home/chalet ○ Hotel/B&B ⊘ Apartment

Austria has some of the finest sites in Europe. In a quiet, rural situation on the edge of the small Reintaler See lake, Seeblick Toni is well worth considering for holidays in the Tirol with many excursions possible. The surrounding mountains give scenic views and the campsite has a neat and tidy appearance. The 243 level pitches (215 for touring units) are in regular rows off hard access roads and are of a good size with firm grass and gravel. All pitches have 10A electricity, 150 are fully serviced including cable TV and phone connections. The large, well appointed restaurant has a roof-top terrace where one can enjoy a meal, drink or snack and admire the lovely scenery. A path leads to the lake for swimming, boating (no sailing or motorboats) and a sunbathing meadow. With a good solarium, sauna, whirlpool and fitness centre, this site provides for an excellent summer holiday and, with ski areas nearby, an excellent winter holiday also. This is a family run site with good English spoken and there is a friendly welcome.

You might like to know

The Topi Club is great fun, and one of the reasons many families return here year after year.

- ☑ Multi-lingual children's club – pre-school
- ☑ Multi-lingual children's club – 5-10 year olds
- ☑ Multi-lingual children's club – 10-14 year olds
- ○ Creative crafts
- ○ Bicycle hire for children
- ☑ Facilities for children in the wash blocks
- ○ Children's pool
- ☑ Children's play area
- ○ Crèche and/or babysitting
- ☑ Local information of interest for children

Facilities
Facilities: The sanitary facilities are of a very high standard, with private cabins and good facilities for disabled visitors. Baby room. Washing machine. Dog shower. Small shop (all year). Bar, restaurant and takeaway (15/5-30/9; Christmas to Easter). Play room. Ski room. Play area. Children's entertainment. Guided walks. Free shuttle bus to ski slopes. Bicycle hire. Slipway for canoes/kayaks. WiFi over site. Off site: Riding 1 km. Indoor pool at Feichten. Pilgrim's Church at Kaltenbrunn. Kaunertaler Glacier.

Open: All year.

Directions: From E60/A12 exit at Landeck and follow the B315 (Reschenpass) turn south onto the B180 signed Bregenz, Arlberg, Innsbruck and Fern Pass for 11 km. to Prutz. Site is signed to the right from the B180 over the bridge.

GPS: 47.08012, 10.6594

Charges guide

Per unit incl. 2 persons
and electricity € 17,00 - € 27,00

extra person € 4,20 - € 7,50

child (5-17 yrs) € 3,80 - € 6,20

dog € 2,00 - € 3,00

Aktiv-Camping Prutz Tirol

Pontlatzstrasse 22, A-6522 Prutz (Tirol)
t: 054 722 648   e: info@aktiv-camping.at
alanrogers.com/AU0155   www.aktiv-camping.at

Accommodation: ☑ Pitch ○ Mobile home/chalet ○ Hotel/B&B ○ Apartment

Aktiv-Camping is a long site which lies beside, but is fenced off from, the River Inn. The 115 touring pitches, mainly gravelled for motorcaravans, are on level ground and average 80 sq.m. They all have 6A electrical connections, adequate water points, and in the larger area fit together somewhat informally. As a result, the site can sometimes have the appearance of being quite crowded. This is an attractive area with many activities in both summer and winter for all age groups. You may well consider using this site not just as an overnight stop, but also for a longer stay. From Roman times onwards, when the Via Augusta passed through, this border region's strategic importance has left behind many fortifications that today feature among its many tourist attractions. Others include rambling, cycling and mountain biking, swimming in lakes and pools as well as interesting, educational and adventurous activities for children. The Tiroler Summer card, available without charge at reception, has free offers and discounts for many attractions; in addition the booklet Wonderful Holiday Bliss, free at reception, contains a wealth of useful tourist information.

You might like to know

A swimming pool complex is just 1.5 km. from the campsite and includes a children's pool and a large sunbathing area.

- ○ Multi-lingual children's club – pre-school
- ○ Multi-lingual children's club – 5-10 year olds
- ○ Multi-lingual children's club – 10-14 year olds
- ☑ Creative crafts
- ○ Bicycle hire for children
- ☑ Facilities for children in the wash blocks
- ○ Children's pool
- ☑ Children's play area
- ○ Crèche and/or babysitting
- ☑ Local information of interest for children

Facilities:
Facilities: Three modern sanitary blocks (the newest in a class of its own) have excellent facilities, including private cabins, underfloor heating and music. Washing machines and dryers. Facilities for disabled visitors. Family bathrooms for hire (some with bathtubs). Motorcaravan services. Well stocked shop. Bar, restaurant and takeaway. Small, heated outdoor pool and children's pool (1/5-15/10). Fitness centre. Two playgrounds, indoor play room and children's cinema. Tennis. Bicycle hire. Watersports and lake swimming. Children's farm and pony rides. New crazy golf course. WiFi over site (charged). Off site: ATM 500 m. Fishing 100 m. Riding 1.5 km. Golf 3 km. Boat launching and sailing 3.5 km. Hiking and skiing (all year). Dry toboggan run at Kaprun 4 km.

Open: All year.

Directions: Site is southwest of Bruck. From road B311, Bruck bypass, take southern exit (Grossglockner) and site is signed from the junction of B311 and B107 roads (small signs). Note: 3.4 m. height restriction if you go through the village.

GPS: 47.2838, 12.81694

Charges guide

Per unit incl. 2 persons and electricity (plus meter) € 23,80 - € 33,90

extra person	€ 5,60 - € 9,00
child (2-10 yrs)	€ 4,40 - € 6,60
dog	€ 3,40 - € 4,60

Special offers for longer stays in low season.

Austria – Bruck

Sportcamp Woferlgut

Kroessenbachstraße 40, A-5671 Bruck an der Glocknerstraße (Salzburg)
t: 065 457 3030   e: info@sportcamp.at
alanrogers.com/AU0180   www.sportcamp.at

Accommodation: ☑ Pitch   ☑ Mobile home/chalet   ☑ Hotel/B&B   ☑ Apartment

The village of Bruck lies at the northern end of the Grossglocknerstrasse spectacular mountain road in the Hohe Tauern National Park, very near the Zeller See. Sportcamp Woferlgut, a family run site, is one of the very best in Austria. Surrounded by mountains, the site is quite flat with pleasant views. The 520 level, grass pitches (300 for touring units) are marked out by shrubs and each has 16A electricity (Europlug), water, drainage, cable TV socket and gas point. A high grass bank separates the site from the road. The site's own lake, used for swimming, is surrounded by a landscaped sunbathing area. A free activity and entertainment programme is provided all year round, but especially during the summer. This includes live music evenings, a club for children, weekly barbecues and guided cycle and mountain tours. The fitness centre has a fully equipped gym, whilst another building contains a sauna and cold dip, Turkish bath, solarium (all free), massage (charged), and a bar. In winter, a cross-country skiing trail and toboggan run lead from the site and a free bus service is provided to nearby skiing facilities.

You might like to know

Woferlgut's Family Experience Adventure Golf is great fun for all the family!

○ Multi-lingual children's club – pre-school
☑ Multi-lingual children's club – 5-10 year olds
☑ Multi-lingual children's club – 10-14 year olds
☑ Creative crafts
☑ Bicycle hire for children
☑ Facilities for children in the wash blocks
☑ Children's pool
☑ Children's play area
○ Crèche and/or babysitting
☑ Local information of interest for children

Facilities:
Facilities: Three exceptionally good quality toilet blocks include washbasins in cabins, facilities for children and disabled visitors, dishwashers and underfloor heating for cool weather. Seven private rooms for rent (3 with jacuzzi baths). Motorcaravan services. Bar. Good restaurant with terrace (May-Oct). Shop (May-Sept). Bowling alley. Disco (July/Aug). TV room. Sauna and solarium. Two play areas (one for under 6s, the other for 6-12 yrs). Bathing and boating on lake. Special entrance rate for lake attractions. Fishing. Bicycle hire. Mountain bike area. Riding. Comprehensive entertainment programmes. Covered stage and outdoor arena for church services (Protestant and Catholic, in German) and folk and modern music concerts. Off site: Mountain walks, climbing and farm visits all in local area.

Open: 27 March - 1 November.

Directions: Döbriach is at the eastern end of the Millstätter See, 15 km. southeast of Spittal. Leave A10 at exit 139 (Spittal, Millstätter) then proceed alongside northern shore of lake through Millstätter towards Döbriach. Just before Döbriach turn right and after 1 km. site is on left.

GPS: 46.77151, 13.64918

Charges guide

Per unit incl. 2 persons and electricity	€ 19,10 - € 34,00
extra person	€ 7,00 - € 10,00
child (4-14 yrs)	€ 5,00 - € 8,00
dog	€ 3,00 - € 4,00

Discounts for retired people in low season.

Komfort-Campingpark Burgstaller

Seefeldstrasse 16, A-9873 Döbriach (Carinthia)
t: 42 467 774 e: info@burgstaller.co.at
alanrogers.com/AU0480 www.komfortcamping.at

Accommodation: ☑ Pitch ☑ Mobile home/chalet ○ Hotel/B&B ☑ Apartment

This is one of Austria's top sites in a beautiful location and with all the amenities you could want. You can always tell a true family run site by the attention to detail and this site oozes perfection. This is an excellent family site with a very friendly atmosphere, particularly in the restaurant in the evenings. Good English is spoken. The 590 pitches (540 for tourers) are on flat, well drained grass, backing onto hedges on either side of access roads. All fully serviced (including WiFi), they vary in size (45-120 sq.m) and there are special pitches for motorcaravans. One pitch actually rotates and follows the sun during the course of the day! The latest sanitary block warrants an architectural award; all toilets have a TV, and a pirate ship on the first floor of the children's area sounds its guns every hour. The site entrance is directly opposite the park leading to the bathing lido, to which campers have free access. There is also a heated swimming pool. Much activity is organised here, including games and competitions for children and there are special Easter and autumn events.

You might like to know

There's some really imaginative entertainment for children, such as searching for precious stones!

- ○ Multi-lingual children's club – pre-school
- ☑ Multi-lingual children's club – 5-10 year olds
- ☑ Multi-lingual children's club – 10-14 year olds
- ☑ Creative crafts
- ○ Bicycle hire for children
- ☑ Facilities for children in the wash blocks
- ○ Children's pool
- ☑ Children's play area
- ○ Crèche and/or babysitting
- ☑ Local information of interest for children

Facilities:
Facilities: Single modern, heated, toilet block includes good sized showers (charged) and vanity style washbasins. Baby room. Basic facilities for disabled campers. Washing machines and dryer. Additional toilet facilities with washbasins in cubicles are located behind the touring field reception building (open July/Aug). Motorcaravan services. Bar and snack bar. Play area. Fun pool for small children. In main park: European and Chinese restaurants, bar and snack bar, takeaways (all year). Shop (Easter-end Aug). Tennis courts and sports field. Water-ski school; water-ski shows (Sundays in July/Aug). Bicycle hire. WiFi throughout (free). Off site: Riding 5 km. Beach 8 km. Golf and sailing 10 km.

Open: All year.

Directions: Jabbeke is 12 km. southwest of Bruges. From A18/A10 motorways, take exit 6/6B (Jabbeke). At roundabout take first exit (site signed). In 650 m. on left-hand bend, turn left to site in 600 m. Main reception is on left but in high season continue to touring site on right in 200 m.

GPS: 51.18448, 3.10445

Charges guide
Per unit incl. up to 4 persons and electricity € 22,00 - € 39,00

dog € 2,00

Recreatiepark Klein Strand

Varsenareweg 29, B-8490 Jabbeke (West Flanders)
t: 050 811 440 e: info@kleinstrand.be
alanrogers.com/BE0555 www.kleinstrand.be

Accommodation: ☑ Pitch ☑ Mobile home/chalet ○ Hotel/B&B ○ Apartment

In a convenient location just off the A10 motorway and close to Bruges, this site is in two distinct areas divided by an access road. The main part of the site offers a lake with a marked off swimming area, a sandy beach, water slides and boating (no fishing). The touring section has 137 large pitches on flat grass separated by well trimmed hedges; all have electricity and access to water and drainage. Some leisure facilities for children are provided on this part of the site, along with a spacious bar and snack bar with takeaway (seasonal). The main site with all the privately owned mobile homes is closer to the lake, so has most of the amenities. These include the main reception building, restaurants, bar, minimarket, and sports facilities. This is a family holiday site and offers a comprehensive programme of activities and entertainment in July and August. Klein Strand is an ideal base from which to visit Bruges (by bus, every 20 minutes) and Gent (by train from Bruges); or why not head for the coast and pick up the delightful KustTram which runs from De Panne near the French border to Knokke?

You might like to know

Klein Strand is within easy reach of some of Belgium's finest seaside resorts, such as Ostende, Zeebrugge and Blankenberge.

- ○ Multi-lingual children's club – pre-school
- ☑ Multi-lingual children's club – 5-10 year olds
- ☑ Multi-lingual children's club – 10-14 year olds
- ☑ Creative crafts
- ○ Bicycle hire for children
- ☑ Facilities for children in the wash blocks
- ☑ Children's pool
- ☑ Children's play area
- ○ Crèche and/or babysitting
- ☑ Local information of interest for children

Facilities: One of the six heated toilet blocks has been fully refitted to a good standard. Some washbasins in cubicles and good hot showers (on payment). Well equipped baby rooms. Facilities for disabled campers. Laundry. Barrier keys can be charged up with units for operating showers, washing machine etc. First aid post. Motorcaravan services. Restaurant (all year, weekends only in winter), takeaway and well stocked shop (Easter-15/9; weekends only). Tennis. Minigolf. Boules. Climbing wall. Playground, trampolines and skateboard ramp. Pedalos, kayaks and bicycles for hire. Children's electric cars and pedal kart tracks (charged for). Free WiFi over site. Off site: Golf 1 km.

Open: All year.

Directions: From E34 Antwerp-Eindhoven take exit 22. On the roundabout take the exit for De Lilse Bergen and follow forest road to site entrance.

GPS: 51.28908, 4.85508

Charges guide

Per unit incl. 4 persons
and electricity € 20,00 - € 26,50

dog € 4,50

Belgium – Gierle

Camping De Lilse Bergen

Strandweg 6, Gierle, B-2275 Lille (Antwerp)
t: 014 557 901   e: info@lilsebergen.be
alanrogers.com/BE0655   www.lilsebergen.be

Accommodation: ☑ Pitch ☑ Mobile home/chalet ○ Hotel/B&B ○ Apartment

This attractive, quietly located holiday site has 513 shady pitches, of which 238 (all with 10A Europlug electricity) are for touring units. Set on sandy soil among pine trees and rhododendrons and arranged around a large lake, the site has a Mediterranean feel. It is well fenced, with a night guard and comprehensive, well labelled, fire-fighting equipment. Cars are parked away from units. The site is really child friendly with each access road labelled with a different animal symbol to enable children to find their own unit easily. An entertainment programme is organised in high season. The lake has marked swimming and diving areas (for adults), a sandy beach, an area for watersports, plus a separate children's pool complex (depth 50 cm) with a most imaginative playground. There are lifeguards and the water meets Blue Flag standards. A building by the lake houses changing rooms, extra toilets, showers and a baby room. There are picnic areas and lakeside and woodland walks.

You might like to know

There is a wealth of fun things to do here, including a tree top adventure course.

- ○ Multi-lingual children's club – pre-school
- ○ Multi-lingual children's club – 5-10 year olds
- ○ Multi-lingual children's club – 10-14 year olds
- ○ Creative crafts
- ○ Bicycle hire for children
- ☑ Facilities for children in the wash blocks
- ○ Children's pool
- ☑ Children's play area
- ○ Crèche and/or babysitting
- ☑ Local information of interest for children

Facilities: Three excellent sanitary units, one new and one heated in winter, include some washbasins in cubicles, facilities for babies and family bathrooms. Facilities for disabled campers. Motorcaravan services. Well stocked shop, bar, restaurant, snack bar and takeaway (all 27/4-1/11). Swimming pools (25/4-13/9). Bicycle hire. Tennis. New playgrounds. Organised activity programme including canoeing, archery, abseiling, mountain biking and climbing (summer). Caving. Fishing (licence essential). Free WiFi over site. Barrier card deposit (€ 20). Max. 1 dog in July/Aug. Off site: Riding 7 km. Golf 25 km.

Open: All year.

Directions: Site is signed north at the roundabout off the N803 Rochefort-St Hubert road at Bure, 8 km. southeast of Rochefort with a narrow, fairly steep, winding descent to site.

GPS: 50.09647, 5.2857

Charges guide

Per unit incl. 2 persons
and electricity € 20,00 - € 36,00

extra person (over 2 yrs) € 4,00 - € 6,00

dog € 4,00 - € 5,00

Belgium – Tellin

Camping Parc la Clusure

Chemin de la Clusure 30, B-6927 Bure-Tellin (Luxembourg)
t: 084 360 050   e: info@parclaclusure.be
alanrogers.com/BE0670   www.parclaclusure.be

Accommodation: ☑ Pitch   ☑ Mobile home/chalet   ○ Hotel/B&B   ○ Apartment

A friendly and very well run site, Parc la Clusure is highly recommended. Set in a river valley in the lovely wooded uplands of the Ardennes, known as the l'Homme Valley touring area, the site has 438 large, marked, grassy pitches (350 for touring). All have access to electricity, cable TV and water taps and are mostly in avenues off a central, tarmac road. There is some noise from the nearby railway. There is a very pleasant riverside walk; the river is shallow in summer and popular with children (caution in winter). The site's heated swimming pool and children's pool have a pool-side bar and terrace. The famous Grottoes of Han are nearby, also the Euro Space Center and Lavaux-Saint Anne castle. Those preferring quieter entertainment might enjoy the Topiary Park at Durbuy.

You might like to know

This is a great base for enjoying the great outdoors. The Ardennes Rangers programme is an action-packed scheme creating opportunities to learn more about the forest, wild animals, the night sky and much more.

- ☑ Multi-lingual children's club – pre-school
- ☑ Multi-lingual children's club – 5-10 year olds
- ○ Multi-lingual children's club – 10-14 year olds
- ☑ Creative crafts
- ○ Bicycle hire for children
- ☑ Facilities for children in the wash blocks
- ☑ Children's pool
- ☑ Children's play area
- ○ Crèche and/or babysitting
- ☑ Local information of interest for children

Facilities: Three sanitary buildings (one new). Covered dishwashing area with hot water. Café/snack bar. Canoe and bicycle hire. Play area. Trampoline. Children's farm. Games room. Activity programme. Accommodation to rent. Free WiFi in bar area. Off site: Villages of Chassepierre and Ste Cécile. Orval Monastery. Walking and cycling trails. Fishing. Riding 2 km. Sedan (Europe's largest castle) 28 km.

Open: 1 April - 1 October.

Directions: Approaching from Brussels (A4), take exit 23A and head for Transinne, Maissin and Paliseul on N899. Continue as far as Menuchenet and then take N89 to Bouillon. Beyond Bouillon take N83 to Florenville and Ste Cécile is 20 km. The site is well signed from here.

GPS: 49.723073, 5.25625

Charges guide

Per unit incl. 2 persons and electricity	€ 24,00 - € 27,00
extra person	€ 4,00
child (3-17 yrs acc to age)	€ 2,50 - € 3,50
dog (max. 1)	€ 2,50

Belgium – Sainte Cécile

Camping de la Semois

Rue de Chassepierre 25, B-6820 Sainte Cécile (Luxembourg)
t: 061 312 187   e: info@campingdelasemois.com
alanrogers.com/BE0714   www.campingdelasemois.be

Accommodation: ☑ Pitch   ☑ Mobile home/chalet   ○ Hotel/B&B   ○ Apartment

La Semois is an attractive family site, located on the banks of the Semois river at the heart of the Belgian Ardennes. This is a tranquil spot and an ideal base for walking, mountain biking and canoeing. The 110 touring pitches are grassy with good shade, but not always level. They are unmarked, but all have 10A electricity. Motorised vehicles are parked at the site entrance to create a tranquil and safe environment. A shallow brook runs through the site and forms a popular play area for children, along with a well equipped playground. The site is most suited to tents and small motorcaravans as the entry road is narrow and steep. Canoeing is very popular and the site owners rent out canoes and will undertake to collect canoeists from points along the river. Mountain bikes are also for rent and maps are available. Children will enjoy the mini-farm with donkeys, goats and Vietnamese pot-bellied pigs. Accommodation to rent on site includes three yurts, two teepees, two large Sahara tents, a Moroccan tent and a Romany-style caravan. There are three sanitary blocks, two of which are basic prefabricated units. The third unit is new and adjoins the reception/bar area.

You might like to know

During high season, there is at least one children's activity a day. These include donkey rides, boat races, archery and a supervised climbing wall.

- ○ Multi-lingual children's club – pre-school
- ○ Multi-lingual children's club – 5-10 year olds
- ○ Multi-lingual children's club – 10-14 year olds
- ○ Creative crafts
- ○ Bicycle hire for children
- ☑ Facilities for children in the wash blocks
- ○ Children's pool
- ☑ Children's play area
- ○ Crèche and/or babysitting
- ☑ Local information of interest for children

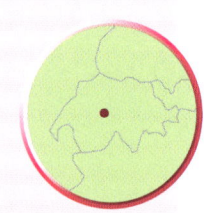

Camping Manor Farm 1

Seestrassee 201, Unterseen, CH-3800 Interlaken-Thunersee (Bern)
t: 033 822 2264 e: info@manorfarm.ch
alanrogers.com/CH9420 www.manorfarm.ch

Accommodation: ☑ Pitch ☑ Mobile home/chalet ○ Hotel/B&B ☑ Apartment

Manor Farm continues to be popular with British and Dutch visitors, being located in one of the traditional touring areas of Switzerland. The flat terrain is divided into 500 individual, numbered pitches, which vary considerably, both in size (40-100 sq.m) and price. There is shade in some places. There are 144 pitches with 4/13A electricity, water and drainage, and 55 also have cable TV connections. Reservations can be made, although you should find space, except perhaps in late July/early August when the best places may be taken. Around 40 per cent of the pitches are taken by permanent or letting units and four tour operators. The site lies outside Interlaken on the northern side of the Thunersee, with most of the site between the road and lake but with one part on the far side of the road. Interlaken is very much a tourist town, but the area is rich in scenery with innumerable mountain excursions and walks available. The lakes and Jungfrau railway are close to hand.

You might like to know

Facilities include children's playgrounds, a large playing field, a volleyball court, four private beaches and watersports activities.

○ Multi-lingual children's club – pre-school
○ Multi-lingual children's club – 5-10 year olds
○ Multi-lingual children's club – 10-14 year olds
☑ Creative crafts
☑ Bicycle hire for children
○ Facilities for children in the wash blocks
☑ Children's pool
☑ Children's play area
○ Crèche and/or babysitting
○ Local information of interest for children

Facilities: Seven separate toilet blocks are practical, heated and fully equipped. They include free hot water for baths and showers. Twenty private toilet units are for rent. Laundry facilities. Motorcaravan services. Gas supplies. Excellent shop (1/4-15/10). Site-owned restaurant adjacent (1/3-30/10). Snack bar with takeaway (1/7-20/8). TV room. Playground and paddling pool. Minigolf. Bicycle hire. Sailing school. Lake swimming. Boat hire (slipway for campers' own boats). Fishing. Daily activity and entertainment programme in high season. Excursions. Max. 1 dog. WiFi in some parts (charged). Off site: Golf (18 holes) 500 m. (handicap card). Riding 3 km. Good area for cycling and walking. Free return bus and boat service to Interlaken's stations and heated indoor and outdoor swimming pools (free entry).

Open: All year.

Directions: Site is 3 km. west of Interlaken along the road running north of the Thunersee towards Thun. From A8 (bypassing Interlaken) take exit 24 (Interlaken West) and follow signs to Camp no. 1.

GPS: 46.68129, 7.81524

Charges guide

Per unit incl. 2 persons and electricity	CHF 35,00 - CHF 62,00
extra person	CHF 5,00 - CHF 10,00
child (6-15 yrs)	CHF 2,50 - CHF 5,00
dog	CHF 2,00 - CHF 4,00

Various discounts for longer stays.

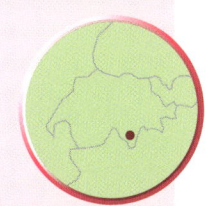

Facilities: The six toilet blocks (three heated) are of exemplary quality. Washing machines and dryers. Motorcaravan services. Gas supplies. Supermarket, restaurant, bar and takeaway (all season). Snack kiosk at beach. Lifeguards on duty. Tennis. Minigolf. Bicycle hire. Canoe and pedalo hire. Boat launching. Playgrounds. Doctor calls. Dogs are not accepted. New chalet for disabled visitors. Camping accessories shop. Car hire. Car wash. WiFi (charged). Off site: Fishing 500 m. Water-skiing and windsurfing 1 km. Riding 5 km. Golf 8 km. Boatyard with maintenance facilities.

Open: 27 March - 31 October.

Directions: On the Bellinzona-Locarno road 13, exit Tenero. Site is signed at Co-op roundabout. Coming from the south, enter Tenero and follow signs to site.

GPS: 46.16895, 8.85592

Charges guide

Per unit incl. 2 persons
and electricity CHF 39,00 - CHF 90,00

extra person CHF 9,00 - CHF 11,00

Some pitches have min. stay regulations. Discounts for stays over 10 days and for seniors.

Switzerland – Tenero

Camping Campofelice

Via alle Brere 7, CH-6598 Tenero (Ticino)
t: 091 745 1417 e: camping@campofelice.ch
alanrogers.com/CH9890 www.campofelice.ch

Accommodation: ☑ Pitch ○ Mobile home/chalet ○ Hotel/B&B ○ Apartment

Considered by many to be the best family campsite in Switzerland, Campofelice is bordered on the front by Lake Maggiore and on one side by the Verzasca estuary, where the site has its own marina. It is divided into rows, with 721 generously sized touring pitches on flat grass on either side of hard access roads. Mostly well shaded, all pitches have electricity connections (10/13A, 360 Europlug) and 410 also have water, drainage and TV connections. Pitches near the lake cost more (these are not available for motorcaravans until September) and a special area is reserved for small tents. A little more expensive than other sites in the area, but excellent value for the range and quality of the facilities. Sporting facilities are good and there are cycle paths in the area, including into Locarno. A free shuttle bus runs to Locarno ferry terminal. The beach by the lake is sandy, long and wider than the usual lakeside ones, and has now been extended, with well kept lawns for sunbathing. It shelves gently so that bathing is safe for children.

You might like to know

There is a tree-top adventure park here, where children can climb in complete safety supervised by qualified instructors.

- ☑ Multi-lingual children's club – pre-school
- ☑ Multi-lingual children's club – 5-10 year olds
- ☑ Multi-lingual children's club – 10-14 year olds
- ☑ Creative crafts
- ☑ Bicycle hire for children
- ○ Facilities for children in the wash blocks
- ○ Children's pool
- ☑ Children's play area
- ○ Crèche and/or babysitting
- ☑ Local information of interest for children

Facilities: The sixteen sanitary blocks are clean and good quality. Facilities for children and baby care areas, some Turkish style WCs, hot showers, with some blocks providing facilities for disabled visitors. Three supermarkets sell most everyday requirements. Fresh fish shop. Four restaurants, bars and snack bars and fast food outlets. Swimming pool and two paddling pools. Sandpit and play areas, with entertainment for all in high season. Tennis. Bicycle hire. Watersports. Boat hire. Minigolf. Riding. Internet café. Jetty and ramp for boats. WiFi (free). Mobile homes for rent (Istria Prestige). Dogs are accepted in certain areas. Off site: Hourly bus service from the reception area. Fishing. Riding 500 m. Golf 2 km. Nearest large supermarket in Novigrad 9 km.

Open: 1 April - 10 October.

Directions: The turn to Lanterna is well signed off the Novigrad to Porec road 8 km. south of Novigrad. Continue for 2 km. along the turn off road towards the coast and the campsite is on the right hand side.

GPS: 45.29672, 13.59442

Charges guide

Per unit incl. 2 persons and electricity	€ 16,90 - € 31,00
with full services	€ 18,30 - € 32,60
extra person	€ 4,40 - € 7,90
child (4-10 yrs)	no charge - € 5,40

Prices for pitches by the sea are higher.

Croatia – *Porec*

Camping Lanterna

Lanterna 1, Tar-Vabriga, HR-52465 Porec (Istria)
t: 052 465 010 e: camping@valamar.com
alanrogers.com/CR6716 www.camping-adriatic.com

Accommodation: ☑ Pitch ☑ Mobile home/chalet ○ Hotel/B&B ○ Apartment

This is a well organised site and one of the largest in Croatia with high standards and an amazing selection of activities, and is part of the Camping on the Adriatic group. Set in 80 hectares with over 3 km. of beach, there are 2,851 pitches, of which 1,887 are for touring units. All have 10A electricity and fresh water, and 225 also have waste water drainage. Pitches are 80-120 sq.m. with some superb locations right on the sea, although these tend to be taken first so it is advisable to book ahead. Some of the better pitches are in a reserved booking area. There are wonderful coastal views from some of the well shaded terraced pitches. Facilities at Lanterna are impressive with the whole operation running smoothly for the campers. The land is sloping in parts and terraced in others. There is a pool complex, including a large pool for children, in addition to the pretty bay with its rocky beaches and buoyed safety areas. Some of the marked and numbered pitches are shaded and arranged to take advantage of the topography. A member of Leading Campings group.

You might like to know

In high season, special events are held in the children's amphitheatre including a mini cinema, a disco, a masked ball and a magic show. Children's clubs cater for youngsters between the ages of 4 and 17 years.

- ☑ Multi-lingual children's club – pre-school
- ☑ Multi-lingual children's club – 5-10 year olds
- ☑ Multi-lingual children's club – 10-14 year olds
- ○ Creative crafts
- ○ Bicycle hire for children
- ☑ Facilities for children in the wash blocks
- ☑ Children's pool
- ☑ Children's play area
- ○ Crèche and/or babysitting
- ☑ Local information of interest for children

Facilities: The sanitary facilities are well maintained with plenty of hot water. Washing machines and dryers. Motorcaravan services. Bar/snack bar. Takeaway food (1/6-15/9). Pool bar. Two restaurants. Aquapark with slide (15/5-15/9). Tennis. Minigolf. Children's entertainment with all major European languages spoken. Bicycle hire. Watersports. Windsurfing school. Trampoline. Miniclub. Games room. Live music (June-Sept). WiFi (charged). Off site: Riding 1 km. Rovinj 3 km. (five buses daily 15/6-15/9). Golf 30 km.

Open: 12 April - 5 October.

Directions: From any access road to Rovinj look for blue signs to AC Polari (amongst other destinations). The site is 3 km. south of Rovinj.

GPS: 45.06286, 13.67489

Charges guide

Per unit incl. 2 persons and electricity € 18,00 - € 56,20	
extra person (18-64 yrs) € 5,40 - € 10,60	
child (5-17 yrs) no charge - € 9,00	
dog € 3,10 - € 8,00	

For stays less than 3 nights in high season add 20%.

Camping Polari

Polari bb, HR-52210 Rovinj (Istria)
t: 052 801 501   e: polari@maistra.hr
alanrogers.com/CR6732   www.campingrovinjvrsar.com

Accommodation: ☑ Pitch   ☑ Mobile home/chalet   ○ Hotel/B&B   ○ Apartment

This 60-hectare site has excellent facilities for both textile and naturist campers, the latter in an area of 12 hectares to the left of the main site. Most parts of the site have good shade cover provided by mature trees. There are 1,650 level pitches for touring units on grass/gravel, terraced in places; many have open views over the sea to the islands. All have access to 10A electricity. An impressive swimming pool complex is child friendly with large paddling areas, and there is a new (2013) aquapark. The ancient town of Rovinj is well worth a visit, and is best reached via the 4.5 km. coastal cycle path or by bus from the campsite. Part of the Maistra group, a massive improvement programme has been undertaken and the result makes it a very attractive site. Enjoy a meal in one of the two restaurants with panoramic views of the sea.

You might like to know

There is a two-kilometre, Blue Flag beach, with rocky areas and stone flats just a few metres from the campsite.

○ Multi-lingual children's club – pre-school
☑ Multi-lingual children's club – 5-10 year olds
○ Multi-lingual children's club – 10-14 year olds
○ Creative crafts
○ Bicycle hire for children
○ Facilities for children in the wash blocks
☑ Children's pool
☑ Children's play area
○ Crèche and/or babysitting
○ Local information of interest for children

Facilities: Five modern and one refurbished toilet blocks with washbasins (some in cabins) and controllable hot showers. Child-size washbasins. Family shower rooms. Facilities for disabled visitors. Outdoor grill station. Motorcaravan services. Car wash. Shopping centre. Restaurants (self-service one has breakfast, lunch and evening menus). Several bars and kiosks. Water play area for children. Outdoor swimming pools. Mini-car track. Riding. Tennis centre. Trim track. Scuba diving. Professional entertainment team. Teen club. Games hall. WiFi. New (2014) beach extension with climbing pyramids. Live shows on stage by the beach. Off site: Historic towns of Zadar (parking difficult) and Nin 3 km.

Open: 25 April - 30 September.

Directions: From Rijeka take no. 2 road south or A1/E65 Autobahn leave at exit for Zadar. Drive north towards Nin, Zaton Holiday Resort is signed a few kilometres before Nin.

GPS: 44.234767, 15.164367

Charges guide

Per unit incl. 2 persons
and electricity € 23,70 - € 55,90

extra person € 6,00 - € 11,90

child (1-11 yrs acc. to age) € 3,30 - € 9,40

dog € 5,00 - € 9,90

Zaton Holiday Resort

Draznikova ulica 76 t, HR-23232 Nin (Dalmatia)
t: 023 280 215 e: camping@zaton.hr
alanrogers.com/CR6782 www.zaton.hr

Accommodation: ☑ Pitch ☑ Mobile home/chalet ◯ Hotel/B&B ☑ Apartment

Zaton Holiday Resort is a modern family holiday park with a one and a half kilometre private sandy beach. It is close to the historic town of Nin and just a few kilometres from the ancient city of Zadar. This park itself is more like a large village and has every amenity one can think of for a holiday on the Dalmatian coast. The village is divided into two areas separated by a public area with reception, bakery, shops, restaurant and a large car park, one for campers close to the sea, the other for a complex with holiday apartments. Zaton has 1,030 mostly level pitches for touring units, all with electricity, water and waste water. All numbered pitches have shade from mature trees and some have views over the extensive, 2 km long sandy beach and the sea. Access is off hard access roads. Zaton caters for everybody's needs on site with numerous bars, restaurants, shops and two swimming pools. Excursions are organised to the Krka waterfalls, the Zrmanja Canyon and the Kornati, Paklenica and Plitvice National Parks. A member of Leading Campings group.

You might like to know

There's a choice of sport and entertainment for children of all ages: pony riding, playground with climbing nets, children's pool etc. The 2 km. long sandy beach has shallow water, ideal for families with younger children.

☑ Multi-lingual children's club – pre-school

☑ Multi-lingual children's club – 5-10 year olds

☑ Multi-lingual children's club – 10-14 year olds

☑ Creative crafts

☑ Bicycle hire for children

☑ Facilities for children in the wash blocks

☑ Children's pool

☑ Children's play area

◯ Crèche and/or babysitting

☑ Local information of interest for children

Facilities: Two modern, attractive and well maintained sanitary blocks, one completely renovated in 2013, have a special children's area and a baby bath. Showers (on payment). Bathrooms to rent. Laundry room with washing machines and dryer. Shop (1/4-30/10). Bar. Restaurant. Takeaway. Indoor heated swimming pool. Sauna, massage and cosmetic studio. Bowling alley. Small zoo. Indoor playroom (free entry). Volleyball. Watersports centre with windsurfing, sailing and catamaran sailing. Go-kart and bicycle hire. WiFi over site and Internet in reception (charged). Off site: Riding 200 m. Golf 8 km. Schwerin Schloss, Wismar (can be reached by cycleway). Rostock and Lübeck.

Open: All year.

Directions: Site is on the coast 6 km. northwest of Wismar. Leave autobahn 20 at exit 8 Wismar Mitte, north to Gägelow then north on minor road to Zierow.

GPS: 53.9347, 11.3718

Charges guide

Per unit incl. 2 persons and electricity	€ 20,30 - € 29,70
extra person	€ 4,50 - € 5,70
child (5-14 yrs)	no charge - € 3,00
dog	€ 3,00

Ostsee-Camping

Strandstrasse 19c, D-23968 Zierow (Mecklenburg-West Pomerania)
t: 038 428 638 20   e: ostseecampingzierow@t-online.de
alanrogers.com/DE25000   www.ostsee-camping.de

Accommodation: ☑ Pitch   ☑ Mobile home/chalet   ○ Hotel/B&B   ☑ Apartment

Set on top of sand dunes overlooking and with direct access to the beach, Ostsee Camping is in a quiet location yet within easy reach of major towns in the region. There is good swimming from the beach, although the site does have a small swimming pool. Of the 486 level pitches, 321 are for touring units, all have electricity connections (10/16A) and 120 are fully serviced. They are set on grass and in places there is some tree shade. Outside the site there are eight quickstop facilities with electricity connections. This is a good site for families, with entertainment programmes in summer, playgrounds and a gently shelving, sandy beach. This part of Germany, formally the DDR, is not that well known to tourists, yet it has a great deal to offer in the way of sandy beaches, attractive landscapes and historic towns, cities and buildings. Anyone travelling to the Baltic coast should make a point of allowing a few hours to visit Schwerin with The Schloss and its gardens, set on an island in the Schweriner lake, the second largest in Northern Germany.

You might like to know

Play areas, indoor swimming pool, bowling alley and watersports are just some of the things that will keep youngsters busy at this family campsite on the Baltic Sea.

- ☑ Multi-lingual children's club – pre-school
- ☑ Multi-lingual children's club – 5-10 year olds
- ☑ Multi-lingual children's club – 10-14 year olds
- ☑ Creative crafts
- ○ Bicycle hire for children
- ☑ Facilities for children in the wash blocks
- ○ Children's pool
- ☑ Children's play area
- ○ Crèche and/or babysitting
- ☑ Local information of interest for children

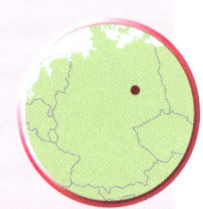

Facilities: Five heated sanitary buildings have first class facilities including showers and both open washbasins and private cabins. Family bathrooms for rent. Facilities for children and disabled campers. Beauty, wellness and cosmetic facilities (April-Oct). Laundry. Motorcaravan services. Shop, bar, restaurants and takeaway (April-Oct). Swimming pool (May-Oct). Sauna. Solarium. Jacuzzi. Sailing, catamaran, windsurfing and diving schools. Boat slipway. Golf courses (18 holes, par 72 and 9 holes, par 3). Riding. Fishing. Archery. Well organised and varied entertainment programmes for all ages. Bicycle hire. Catamaran hire. WiFi over part of site (charged). Off site: Naturist beach 500 m.

Open: All year.

Directions: From Hamburg take A1/E47 north towards Puttgarden, after crossing the bridge to Fehmarn first exit to the right to Avendorf. In Avendorf turn left and follow the signs for Wulfen and the site.
GPS: 54.40805, 11.17374

Charges guide

Per unit incl. 2 persons and electricity	€ 17,80 - € 43,50
extra person	€ 5,00 - € 9,30
child (2-12 yrs)	€ 2,60 - € 5,20
dog	€ 3,00 - € 7,50

Plus surcharges for larger pitches. Many discounts available and special family prices.

Germany – Wulfen

Camping Wulfener Hals

Wulfener Hals Weg 100, D-23769 Wulfen auf Fehmarn (Schleswig-Holstein)
t: 043 718 6280   e: info@wulfenerhals.de
alanrogers.com/DE30030   www.wulfenerhals.de

Accommodation: ☑ Pitch   ☑ Mobile home/chalet   ○ Hotel/B&B   ☑ Apartment

This is a top class, all year round site suitable as a stopover or as a base for a longer stay. Attractively situated by the sea, it is large, mature (34 hectares) and well maintained. It has over 800 individual pitches (half for touring) of up to 160 sq.m. in glades. Some are separated by bushes providing shade in the older parts, less so in the newer areas nearer the sea. There are many hardstandings and all pitches have electricity, water and drainage. Some new rental accommodation has been added, including a 'honeymoon mobile home'. A separate area has been developed for motorcaravans. It provides 60 extra large pitches, all with electricity, water and drainage, and some with TV aerial points, together with a new toilet block. There is much to do for young and old alike at Wulfener Hals, with a new heated outdoor pool and paddling pool (unsupervised), although the sea is naturally popular as well. The site also has many sporting facilities including its own golf courses and schools for watersports. A member of Leading Campings group.

You might like to know

Amenities for children include a trampoline, a bouncy castle, hire of 'Dino cars' in different sizes, minigolf and Bambini surf lessons (5 yrs). There are inclusive packages for young children (high chair, baby bath etc) and babysitting by arrangement.

- ☑ Multi-lingual children's club – pre-school
- ☑ Multi-lingual children's club – 5-10 year olds
- ☑ Multi-lingual children's club – 10-14 year olds
- ☑ Creative crafts
- ☑ Bicycle hire for children
- ☑ Facilities for children in the wash blocks
- ☑ Children's pool
- ☑ Children's play area
- ☑ Crèche and/or babysitting
- ☑ Local information of interest for children

Facilities: Heated sanitary blocks provide free showers. Child-sized toilets and showers. Baby rooms. Facilities for disabled visitors. Laundry facilities. Motorcaravan services. Shop. Bar, restaurant and snack bar. Open-air stage and soundproofed disco. Wellness, solarium and sauna. Archery. Watersports. Minigolf. Bouncy castles. Internet café. Beach fishing. Riding. WiFi (charged). Off site: Boat launching 6 km. Golf 16 km.

Open: 1 April - 26 October.

Directions: After crossing the bridge follow road to Landkirchen and Petersdorf. From Petersdorf site is signed. It is 4 km. northwest of the town.

GPS: 54.48761, 11.0186

Charges guide

Per unit incl. 2 persons
and electricity € 18,20 - € 36,90

child (under 17 yrs) € 2,00 - € 6,00

extra person € 4,10 - € 7,70

No credit cards.

Strandcamping Wallnau

Wallnau 1, D-23769 Fehmarn (Schleswig-Holstein)
t: 043 729 456 e: wallnau@strandcamping.de
alanrogers.com/DE30070 www.strandcamping.de

Accommodation: ☑ Pitch ☑ Mobile home/chalet ○ Hotel/B&B ○ Apartment

With direct beach access and protected from the wind by a dyke, this family site is on Germany's second largest island (since 1963 joined to the Baltic sea coast by a bridge). This is a quiet location on the western part of Fehmarn Island in close proximity to a large bird sanctuary. Of the 800 pitches, 400 are for touring, all with electricity (6/16A) and on level grass areas arranged in alleys and separated by hedges. The island is low lying, ideal for leisurely walking and cycling, especially along the track that runs along the top of the dyke. The beach is a mixture of sand and pebbles, and in summer lifeguards are on duty. The southern part is a naturist area. For those with an ornithological interest, the bird sanctuary with over 80 species is worth visiting. Swimming, sailing and diving are possible in the sea and there is a windsurfing school. For those who prefer dry land there is pony riding for children and a riding school. During summer there are entertainment programmes for children and courses for adults; twice a week there are film shows.

You might like to know

Riding is popular here, with opportunities for all ages.

○ Multi-lingual children's club – pre-school
☑ Multi-lingual children's club – 5-10 year olds
☑ Multi-lingual children's club – 10-14 year olds
☑ Creative crafts
○ Bicycle hire for children
☑ Facilities for children in the wash blocks
○ Children's pool
☑ Children's play area
○ Crèche and/or babysitting
☑ Local information of interest for children

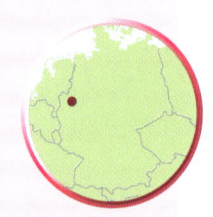

Erholungszentrum Grav-Insel

Grav-Insel 1, D-46487 Wesel (North Rhine-Westphalia)
t: 028 197 2830 e: info@grav-insel.com
alanrogers.com/DE32020 www.grav-insel.de

Accommodation: ☑ Pitch ☑ Mobile home/chalet ○ Hotel/B&B ○ Apartment

Grav-Insel claims to be the largest family camping site in Germany, providing entertainment and activities to match, with over 2,000 permanent units. A section for 500 touring units runs beside the water to the left of the entrance and this area has been completely renewed. These pitches, all with 10A electricity, are flat, grassy, mostly without shade and of about 100 sq.m. A walk through the site takes you past a nature reserve and to the Rhine, where you can watch the barges. Despite its size, this site is very well maintained, calm, clean and spacious and this is down to the family who started it 40 years ago. This site, on the border with Holland, is an excellent stop over for the north and east of Germany. However, once here, you may decide to stay longer to take advantage of the excellent restaurant (special evenings each week), birdwatching on the private reserve or to visit Xanten with its Roman amphitheatre in the archaeological park.

You might like to know

Child care services are available and there is a petting zoo on site for youngsters to enjoy.

○ Multi-lingual children's club – pre-school
☑ Multi-lingual children's club – 5-10 year olds
○ Multi-lingual children's club – 10-14 year olds
○ Creative crafts
☑ Bicycle hire for children
☑ Facilities for children in the wash blocks
○ Children's pool
☑ Children's play area
○ Crèche and/or babysitting
○ Local information of interest for children

Facilities: Excellent sanitary facilities, all housed in a modern building above which is the bar/restaurant (open all year). Touring area augmented by prefabricated units to be renewed. Facilities for disabled visitors. Baby room. Launderette. Motorcaravan services. Large supermarket. Restaurant/pizzeria. Entertainment area with satellite TV. WiFi. Solarium. Large play area on sand plus wet weather indoor area. Bicycle hire. Boat park. Sailing. Fishing. Swimming. Football (international coaching in high season). Entertainment in high season. Off site: Bus service 500 m. Riding 2 km. The attractive town of Xanten 23 km. Nord Park Duisburg, where an old steelworks has been turned into a leisure complex 25 km. Kleve (Cleves) – birthplace of Anne of Cleves 30 km. Warner Bros Movie Park, Bottrop 30 km.

Open: All year.

Directions: Site is 5 km. northwest of Wesel. From A3 take exit 6 and B58 towards Wesel, then right towards Rees. Turn left at sign for Flüren, through Flüren and left to site after 1.5 km. If approaching Wesel from west (B58), cross the Rhine, turn left at first traffic lights and follow signs Grav-Insel and Flüren.

GPS: 51.67062, 6.55600

Charges guide

Per unit incl. 2 persons and electricity	€ 15,50
extra person	€ 3,00
child (under 12 yrs)	€ 1,50
dog	€ 1,50

Facilities: Three good quality sanitary blocks can be heated and have free showers, washbasins (open and in cabins), baby rooms and facilities for wheelchair users. Laundry. Motorcaravan services. Café and shop (both summer only). Restaurant by entrance open all day (closed Feb). Watersports. Boat and bicycle hire. Lake swimming. Fishing. Minigolf. Playground. Sauna. Solarium. Disco (high season). Internet access. Off site: New national park opposite site entrance. Riding 500 m. Golf 25 km. Cable car (bicycles accepted). Aquapark. Boat trips on the Edersee.

Open: All year.

Directions: Site is 45 km. southwest of Kassel. From A44 Oberhausen-Kassel autobahn, take exit 64 for Diemelstadt and head south for Korbach. Site is between Korbach and Frankenberg on the B252 road, 1 km. to the south of Herzhausen at the pedestrian traffic lights.

GPS: 51.17550, 8.89067

Charges guide

Per unit incl. 2 persons and electricity	€ 26,00 - € 30,50
extra person	€ 5,90 - € 7,50
child (3-15 yrs)	€ 3,50 - € 4,40
dog	€ 3,60

Germany – Vöhl

Camping & Ferienpark Teichmann

Zum Träumen 1A, D-34516 Vöhl-Herzhausen (Hessen)
t: 056 352 45   e: info@camping-teichmann.de
alanrogers.com/DE32800   www.camping-teichmann.de

Accommodation: ☑ Pitch ☑ Mobile home/chalet ○ Hotel/B&B ○ Apartment

Situated near the eastern end of the 27 km. long Edersee and the Kellerwald-Edersee National Park, this attractively set site is surrounded by wooded hills and encircles a six-hectare lake, which has separate areas for swimming, fishing and boating. Of the 500 pitches, 250 are for touring; all have 10A electricity and 50 have fresh and waste water connections. The pitches are on level grass, some having an area of hardstanding, and are separated by hedges and mature trees. At the opposite side of the lake from the entrance, there is a separate area for tents with its own sanitary block. The adjoining national park, a popular leisure attraction, offers a wealth of holiday/sporting activities including walking, cycling (there are two passenger ferries that take cycles), boat trips, cable car and much more. Full details are available at the friendly reception. For winter sports lovers, the ski centre at Winterberg is only 30 km. away from this all-year-round site.

You might like to know

The sauna and solarium are a great way to relax after enjoying a guided walk or a bike ride along one of the superb cycle routes.

○ Multi-lingual children's club – pre-school
○ Multi-lingual children's club – 5-10 year olds
○ Multi-lingual children's club – 10-14 year olds
○ Creative crafts
☑ Bicycle hire for children
☑ Facilities for children in the wash blocks
○ Children's pool
☑ Children's play area
○ Crèche and/or babysitting
○ Local information of interest for children

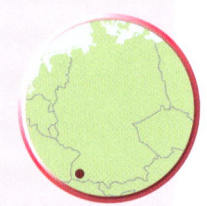

Ferien-Campingplatz Münstertal

Dietzelbachstrasse 6, D-79244 Münstertal (Baden-Württemberg)
t: 076 367 080   e: info@camping-muenstertal.de
alanrogers.com/DE34500   www.camping-muenstertal.de

Accommodation: ☑ Pitch ○ Mobile home/chalet ○ Hotel/B&B ☑ Apartment

Münstertal is an impressive site pleasantly situated in a valley on the western edge of the Black Forest. It has been one of the top graded sites in Germany for 25 years, and first time visitors will soon realise why when they see the standard of the facilities here. There are 305 individual pitches in two areas, either side of the entrance road on flat gravel, their size varying from 70-100 sq.m. All have electricity (16A), water and drainage; some have TV and radio connections. The large indoor pool and the outdoor pool, are both heated and free. The adjacent Health and Fitness Centre offers a range of treatments. Children are very well catered for here with a play area and play equipment, tennis courts, minigolf, a games room with table tennis, table football and a pool table, and fishing. Riding is popular and the site has its own stables. There is a winter ice rink for skating and ice hockey. The site organises regular guided walks and cycle rides, plus winter sports and cross-country skiing (there are courses in winter for both children and adults, and ski hire).

Facilities: Three toilet blocks are of truly first class quality, with washbasins, all in cabins, showers with full glass dividers, baby bath, a unit for disabled visitors and individual bathrooms, some for hire. Dishwashers in two blocks. Laundry. Drying room. Motorcaravan services. Well stocked shop (all year). Restaurant, particularly good (closed Nov). Heated swimming pools, indoor all year, outdoor (with children's area). New health and fitness centre. Sauna and solarium. Games room. Extensive playing fields. Fishing. Bicycle hire. Tennis courses in summer. Riding. Ice rink (in winter). WiFi over site (charged). Konus Card for free bus and train travel. Off site: Village amenities and train station next to site entrance. Golf 15 km. Freiburg and Basel easy driving distances for day trips.

Open: All year.

Directions: Münstertal is south of Freiburg. From A5 autobahn take exit 64, turn southeast via Bad Krozingen and Staufen and continue 5 km. to the start of Münstertal, where site is signed from the main road on the left.
GPS: 47.85973, 7.76375

Charges guide

Per unit incl. 2 persons and services	€ 25,00 - € 28,50
extra person	€ 7,10 - € 8,70
child (2-10 yrs)	€ 4,80 - € 5,50
dog	€ 3,50

Maestro cards accepted.

You might like to know

Bicycles can be hired on site (for both adults and children) – there is no better way to explore the Black Forest.

○ Multi-lingual children's club – pre-school
☑ Multi-lingual children's club – 5-10 year olds
☑ Multi-lingual children's club – 10-14 year olds
○ Creative crafts
☑ Bicycle hire for children
☑ Facilities for children in the wash blocks
☑ Children's pool
☑ Children's play area
○ Crèche and/or babysitting
☑ Local information of interest for children

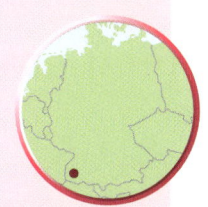

Facilities: Three good quality, heated sanitary blocks include some washbasins in cabins. Baby room. Facilities for disabled visitors. Laundry facilities. Motorcaravan services. Shop. Excellent restaurant. Takeaway (weekends and daily in high season). Wellness centre. Indoor/outdoor pool. Community room with TV. Activity programme (high season). Play areas. Boules. Tennis. Fishing. Minigolf. Barbecue. Beach bar. Petting zoo and aviary. Electric go-karts. Bicycle hire. Free WiFi in central area. Off site: Riding 1.5 km. Golf 5 km. Neuenburg, Breisach, Freiburg, Basel and the Black Forest.

Open: All year.

Directions: From autobahn A5 take Neuenburg exit, turn left, then almost immediately left at traffic lights, left at next junction and follow signs for 2 km. to site (called 'Neuenburg' on most signs).

GPS: 47.79693, 7.55

Charges guide

Per unit incl. 2 persons and electricity € 26,00	
extra person € 6,50	
child (2-15 yrs) € 3,50	
dog € 3,00	

Discount every 10th night.

Germany – Neuenburg

Gugel's Dreiländer Camping

Oberer Wald 3, D-79395 Neuenburg am Rhein (Baden-Württemberg)
t: 076 317 719 e: info@camping-gugel.de
alanrogers.com/DE34550 www.camping-gugel.de

Accommodation: ☑ Pitch ☑ Mobile home/chalet ○ Hotel/B&B ○ Apartment

Set in natural heath and woodland, Gugel's is an attractive site with 220 touring pitches, either in small clearings in the trees, in open areas or on a hardstanding section used for overnight stays. All have electricity (10/16A), and 40 also have water, waste water and satellite TV connections. Opposite is a meadow where late arrivals and early departures may spend the night. There may be some road noise near the entrance. The site may become very busy in high season and on bank holidays but you should always find room. The excellent pool and wellness complex add to the attraction of this all year site. There is a social room with satellite TV where guests are welcomed with a glass of wine and a slide presentation of the attractions of the area. The Rhine is within walking distance and there is an extensive programme of activities on offer for all ages. The site is ideally placed not only for enjoying and exploring the south of the Black Forest, but also for night stops when travelling from Frankfurt to Basel on the A5 autobahn.

You might like to know

The family entertainment programme runs during July and August, offering competitions, barbecues, handicrafts, family games, karaoke and excursions.

○ Multi-lingual children's club – pre-school
☑ Multi-lingual children's club – 5-10 year olds
☑ Multi-lingual children's club – 10-14 year olds
☑ Creative crafts
○ Bicycle hire for children
☑ Facilities for children in the wash blocks
☑ Children's pool
☑ Children's play area
○ Crèche and/or babysitting
○ Local information of interest for children

Strandcamping Waging am See

Am See 1, D-83329 Waging-am-See (Bavaria (S))
t: 086 815 52   e: info@strandcamp.de
alanrogers.com/DE36860   www.strandcamp.de

Accommodation: ☑ Pitch   ○ Mobile home/chalet   ○ Hotel/B&B   ☑ Apartment

Facilities: Good sanitary facilities include private cabins and free showers. Facilities for disabled visitors and children in the four modern blocks. 11 private bathrooms for rent. Laundry facilities. Motorcaravan services. Shop and Internet access at reception. Very good restaurant and bar. Lake beach. Windsurfing. Tennis. Archery. Minigolf. Fishing. Bicycle and electric bike hire. WiFi over site (charged). A new 200 sq.m. indoor children's play area and a young person's games room and trampoline have been added. Off site: Golf 1 km. Berchtesgaden. Salzberg. Chiemsee palace and gardens (boats depart from Prien).

Open: All year.

Directions: Site is 30 km. northwest of Salzburg. From A8 take exit 112 and head towards Traunstein. Turn right on road no. 304 then left towards Waging. Just before bridge turn right and then right towards site.

GPS: 47.9434, 12.7475

Charges guide

Per unit incl. 2 persons
and electricity € 20,70 - € 39,70

extra person € 5,90 - € 7,90
child (3-15 yrs) € 3,50 - € 3,90
dog € 3,50 - € 3,90

This is an exceptionally big site on the banks of a large lake fed by clear alpine streams. There are some 700 pitches for touring units out of a total of over 1,200. All the grass, level touring pitches have electricity (16A) with 150 also providing water and drainage and some new 150 sq.m. super comfort pitches. As you would expect with a site of this kind, there is a considerable range of sports facilities and an extensive games and entertainment programme during July and August. A small sandy beach offers facilities for swimming in the lake (lifeguards are in attendance in the high season). An adjoining windsurfing school is available to campers. The site has a large restaurant and beer garden on the banks of the lake and rooms and caravans available to rent. A member of Leading Campings group.

You might like to know

High season activities include a torchlight walk, mini disco, barbecue evening and a weekly trip to an amusement park, zoo or child-friendly Museum. Soccer training for children with former professionals and internationals, Dieter Eckstein and Werner Lorant.

☑ Multi-lingual children's club – pre-school

☑ Multi-lingual children's club – 5-10 year olds

☑ Multi-lingual children's club – 10-14 year olds

☑ Creative crafts

☑ Bicycle hire for children

☑ Facilities for children in the wash blocks

○ Children's pool

☑ Children's play area

○ Crèche and/or babysitting

☑ Local information of interest for children

Camping Hopfensee

Fischerbichl 17, D-87629 Füssen im Allgäu (Bavaria (S))
t: 083 629 17710 e: info@camping-hopfensee.de
alanrogers.com/DE36700 www.camping-hopfensee.com

Accommodation: ☑ Pitch ☑ Mobile home/chalet ○ Hotel/B&B ○ Apartment

This exceptional, family run site is situated beside a lake in the beautiful Bavarian Alps, not far from the fairytale castle of Neuschwanstein. Although one can appreciate the mountain scenery from the 376 level, fully serviced pitches, it is more comfortably viewed whilst swimming in the 31 degree swimming pool on the first floor of the wellness complex. The wellness complex, which offers a full spa programme and excellent sanitary facilities, is arranged around a large courtyard adorned with cascading flowers. The site has an excellent restaurant and bar with views over the lake. The site is a comfortable base for summer tours and sightseeing in the Bavarian Alps. During winter or in bad weather the site has a full range of facilities under cover that include a cinema and 1,000 sq.m. play room/barn on two levels. Apart from the many colourful displays of flowers that decorate the site, colour is also provided by the glass doors and windows, created by the owner's daughter, throughout the spa complex. A member of Leading Campings Group.

You might like to know

There's an excellent indoor play area here – ideal for football, volleyball and basketball – with a giant slide!

- ○ Multi-lingual children's club – pre-school
- ○ Multi-lingual children's club – 5-10 year olds
- ○ Multi-lingual children's club – 10-14 year olds
- ○ Creative crafts
- ○ Bicycle hire for children
- ☑ Facilities for children in the wash blocks
- ○ Children's pool
- ☑ Children's play area
- ☑ Crèche and/or babysitting
- ☑ Local information of interest for children

Facilities: The excellent heated sanitary facilities provide free hot water in washbasins (some in cabins) and large showers. Separate babies' and children's washrooms. Private units for rent. Motorcaravan services. Takeaway. Shop. Supervised courses of water treatments, aromatherapy, massage, etc. Sauna, solarium and steam bath. Playground and kindergarten. Pavilion for children (up to 6 yrs old, accompanied by adult) and meeting room for teenagers. Large games room. Bicycle hire. Tennis. Fishing. Ski safari in winter. Small golf academy and discounts for two local courses. No tents taken. Off site: Riding and boat launching 1 km.

Open: 16 December - 4 November.

Directions: Site is 4 km. north of Füssen. Turn off B16 to Hopfen and site is on the left through a car park. If approaching from the west on B310, turn towards Füssen at T-junction with the B16 and immediately right again for the road to Hopfen.
GPS: 47.60572, 10.68052

Charges guide

Per unit incl. 2 persons and electricity
(plus meter) € 30,35 - € 34,20

extra person € 8,85 - € 10,10

child (2-18 yrs acc. to age)
€ 5,40 - € 9,55

dog € 4,15

Special offers that include wellness programmes. No credit cards.

Facilities: The first class toilet block has underfloor heating, washbasins in cabins and private units with WC, shower, basin and bidet for rent. Unit for disabled guests with the latest facilities. Baby bath, dog bathroom and a heated room for ski equipment (with lockers). Washing machines, free dryers and irons. Gas supplies. Motorcaravan services. Cooking facilities. Shop. Restaurants (waiter, self-service and takeaway). Bar. Youth room. Solarium. Bicycle hire. Playground. WiFi (charged). Organised activities and excursions. Bus service to ski slopes in winter. Off site: Fishing 400 m. Riding and golf 3 km. Discounted entry at Alpspitz-Wellenbad in Garmisch-Partenkirchen and Karwendel Bad in Mittenwald.

Open: All year excl. 6 November - 15 December.

Directions: Site is just off main Garmisch-Partenkirchen-Innsbruck road no. 2 between Klais and Krün, 15 km. from Garmisch watch for small sign Tennsee & Barmsee and turn right there for site.

GPS: 47.49066, 11.25396

Charges guide

Per unit incl. 2 persons	€ 23,00 - € 26,00
extra person	€ 7,50 - € 8,00
child (6-16 yrs)	€ 3,00 - € 4,00
electricity (per kWh)	€ 0,75
dog	€ 3,30

Senior citizens special rates (not winter).

Germany – Krün-Obb

Alpen-Caravanpark Tennsee

Am Tennsee 1, D-82494 Krün-Obb (Bavaria (S))
t: 088 251 70   e: info@camping-tennsee.de
alanrogers.com/DE36800   www.camping-tennsee.de

Accommodation: ☑ Pitch   ○ Mobile home/chalet   ○ Hotel/B&B   ☑ Apartment

Tennsee is an excellent, friendly site in truly beautiful surroundings high up (1,000 m) in the Karwendel Alps with super mountain views, and close to many famous places of which Innsbruck (44 km) and Oberammergau (26 km) are two. Mountain walks are plentiful, with several lifts close by. It is an attractive site with good facilities including 164 serviced pitches with individual connections for electricity (up to 16A and two connections), gas, TV, radio, telephone, water and waste water. The other 80 pitches all have electricity and some of these are available for overnight guests at a reduced rate. Reception and comfortable restaurants, a bar, cellar youth room and a well stocked shop are all housed in attractive buildings. Many activities and excursions are organised to local attractions by the Zick family, who run the site in a very friendly, helpful and efficient manner.

You might like to know

The fairytale castle of Neuschwanstein makes for a fantastic day out and is just over an hour's drive from the site.

○ Multi-lingual children's club – pre-school
☑ Multi-lingual children's club – 5-10 year olds
○ Multi-lingual children's club – 10-14 year olds
☑ Creative crafts
○ Bicycle hire for children
○ Facilities for children in the wash blocks
○ Children's pool
☑ Children's play area
☑ Crèche and/or babysitting
☑ Local information of interest for children

Facilities: Two excellent buildings provide modern, heated facilities with private cabins, a family room, baby room, units for disabled visitors and eight bathrooms for hire. Special facilities for children with novelty showers and washbasins. Jacuzzi. Kitchen. Gas supplies. Motorcaravan services. Shop, bar (1/3-31/12) plus restaurant (15/3-31/12). Bicycle hire. Lake swimming. Sports field. Fishing. Play area. Sauna. Train, bus and theatre tickets from reception. Internet point. WiFi throughout (charged). Minigolf. Fitness room. Regular guided bus trips to Dresden, Prague etc. Off site: Riding next door (lessons available). Public transport to Dresden 1 km. Golf 7.5 km. Nearby dinosaur park, zoo and indoor karting.

Open: All year excl. February.

Directions: Site is 17 km. northeast of Dresden. From the A4 (Dresden-Görlitz) take exit 85 (Pulnitz) and travel south towards Radeberg. Pass through Leppersdorf and site is signed to the left. Follow signs for Kleinröhrsdorf and camping. Site is 4 km. from the autobahn exit.

GPS: 51.120401, 13.980103

Charges guide

Per unit incl. 2 persons
and electricity € 19,90 - € 26,60

extra person € 5,00 - € 8,00

child (3-15 yrs acc. to age)
€ 2,50 - € 4,50

dog € 2,50 - € 3,50

Various special offers in low season.

Germany – Dresden

Camping & Freizeitpark LuxOase

Arnsdorfer Strasse 1, Kleinröhrsdorf, D-01900 Dresden (Saxony)
t: 035 952 56666 e: info@luxoase.de
alanrogers.com/DE38330 www.luxoase.de

Accommodation: ☑ Pitch ○ Mobile home/chalet ○ Hotel/B&B ☑ Apartment

This is a well organised and quiet site located just north of Dresden with easy access from the autobahn. The site has very good facilities and is arranged on grassland beside a lake. There is access from the site to the lake through a gate. Although the site is fairly open, trees do provide shade in some areas. There are 198 large touring pitches (plus 40 seasonal in a separate area), marked by bushes or posts on generally flat or slightly sloping grass. All have 10/16A electricity and 132 have water and drainage. At the entrance is an area of hardstanding (with electricity) for late arrivals. A brand new building provides excellent sanitary facilities, a separate washing area for children with showers in a castle and washbasins in a steam river boat which blows soap bubbles in the evening. A wellness centre includes a pool and saunas, massages, a fitness room and indoor playground for children. You may swim, fish or use inflatables in the lake. A wide entertainment programme is organised for children in high season. A member of Leading Campings group.

You might like to know

Tickets for local excursions are available from the campsite reception.

- ☑ Multi-lingual children's club – pre-school
- ☑ Multi-lingual children's club – 5-10 year olds
- ☑ Multi-lingual children's club – 10-14 year olds
- ☑ Creative crafts
- ☑ Bicycle hire for children
- ☑ Facilities for children in the wash blocks
- ○ Children's pool
- ☑ Children's play area
- ○ Crèche and/or babysitting
- ☑ Local information of interest for children

Hvidbjerg Strand Camping

Hvidbjerg Strandvej 27, DK-6857 Blavand (Ribe)
t: 75 27 90 40 e: info@hvidbjerg.dk
alanrogers.com/DK2010 www.hvidbjerg.dk

Accommodation: ☑ Pitch ☑ Mobile home/chalet ○ Hotel/B&B ○ Apartment

A family owned TopCamp holiday site, Hvidbjerg Strand is on the west coast near Blåvands Huk, 43 km. from Esbjerg. It is a high quality, seaside site with a wide range of amenities including a large wellness facility. Most of the 570 pitches have electricity (6/10A) and the 130 'comfort' pitches also have water, drainage and satellite TV. To the rear of the site, 70 new, fully serviced pitches have been developed, some up to 250 sq.m. and 44 with private sanitary facilities. Most pitches are individual and divided by hedges, in rows on flat sandy grass, with areas also divided by small trees and hedges. On-site leisure facilities include an indoor suite of supervised playrooms designed for all ages, with Lego, computers, video games, TV, etc. and an impressive, tropical-style indoor pool complex. This includes stalactite caves and a 70 m. water chute, the 'black hole' with sounds and lights, plus water slides, spa baths, Turkish bath and a sauna. A Blue Flag beach and windsurfing school are adjacent to the site and the town offers a full activity programme during high season. A member of Leading Campings group.

You might like to know

Legoland is always great fun and makes a great day trip from the site.

- ☑ Multi-lingual children's club – pre-school
- ☑ Multi-lingual children's club – 5-10 year olds
- ☑ Multi-lingual children's club – 10-14 year olds
- ☑ Creative crafts
- ○ Bicycle hire for children
- ☑ Facilities for children in the wash blocks
- ☑ Children's pool
- ☑ Children's play area
- ○ Crèche and/or babysitting
- ☑ Local information of interest for children

Facilities: Five superb toilet units include washbasins, roomy showers, spa baths, suites for disabled visitors, family bathrooms, kitchens and laundry facilities. Bathroom for children decorated with dinosaurs and Disney characters, and racing car baby baths. Motorcaravan services. Supermarket. Café/restaurant. TV rooms. Pool complex, solarium and sauna. Wellness facility. Western-themed indoor play hall. Play areas. Supervised play rooms (09.00-16.00 daily). Barbecue areas. Minigolf. Riding (Western style). Fishing. Dog showers. ATM machine. Free WiFi. Off site: Legoland 70 km.

Open: 20 March - 18 October.

Directions: From Varde take roads 181/431 to Blåvand. Site is signed left on entering the town.

GPS: 55.54600, 8.13507

Charges guide

Per unit incl. 2 persons and electricity € 33,80 - € 61,80	
extra person € 10,90	
child (0-11 yrs) € 8,10	
dog € 4,00	

Facilities: Four good sanitary units are cleaned three times daily. Facilities include washbasins in cubicles or with divider/curtain, family and whirlpool bathrooms (on payment), suites for babies and disabled visitors. Free sauna. Superb kitchens and a fully equipped laundry. Supermarket (1/4-1/11). Restaurant. Bar. Café, takeaway. Pool complex with spa facilities. Bowling. Minigolf. Tennis. Go-karts and other outdoor sports. Children's 'playworld'. Playgrounds. Pets corner. Golf. Fishing pond. Practice golf (3 holes). Off site: Beach and riding 2 km. Bicycle hire 6 km.

Open: All year.

Directions: From south or north, take road 26 to Salling Sund bridge, site is signed Jesperhus, just north of the bridge.
GPS: 56.75082, 8.81580

Charges guide

Per person	DKK 80
child (1-11 yrs)	DKK 60
pitch no charge -	DKK 50
electricity	DKK 40

Jesperhus Feriecenter & Camping

Legindvej 30, DK-7900 Nykobing Mors (Viborg)
t: **96 70 14 00** e: **jesperhus@jesperhus.dk**
alanrogers.com/DK2140 www.jesperhus.dk

Accommodation: ☑ Pitch ☑ Mobile home/chalet ○ Hotel/B&B ○ Apartment

Jesperhus is an extensive, well organised and busy site with many leisure activities, adjacent to Blomsterpark (Northern Europe's largest flower park). This TopCamp site has 662 numbered pitches, mostly in rows with some terracing, divided by shrubs and trees and with shade in parts. Many pitches are taken by seasonal, tour operator or rental units, so advance booking is advised for peak periods. Electricity (6A) is available on all pitches and water points are in all areas. There are 300 pitches available with full services. With all the activities at this site, an entire holiday could be spent here regardless of the weather, although Jesperhus is also an excellent centre for touring. The indoor and outdoor pool complex has three pools, diving boards, water slides with the 'black hole', spa pools, saunas and a solarium. Although it may appear to be just part of Jutland, Mors is an island in its own right surrounded by the lovely Limfjord. It is joined to the mainland by a 2,000 m. bridge at the end of which are signs to Blomsterpark (which also houses Butterfly World, a bird zoo, terrarium and aquarium) and the campsite – both under the same ownership.

You might like to know

The Flower Park is the largest of its kind in Northern Europe and features a zoo and an amusement park.

- ○ Multi-lingual children's club – pre-school
- ○ Multi-lingual children's club – 5-10 year olds
- ○ Multi-lingual children's club – 10-14 year olds
- ☑ Creative crafts
- ☑ Bicycle hire for children
- ☑ Facilities for children in the wash blocks
- ☑ Children's pool
- ☑ Children's play area
- ○ Crèche and/or babysitting
- ○ Local information of interest for children

Facilities

Facilities: Two good, large, heated toilet blocks are central, with spacious showers and some washbasins in cubicles. Separate room for children. Baby rooms. Bathrooms for families (some charged) and disabled visitors. Laundry. Well equipped kitchens and barbecue areas. TV lounges. Motorcaravan services. Pizzeria. Supermarket, restaurant and bar (all season). Pool complex. Wellness centre with sauna, solariums, whirlpool bath, fitness room and indoor play hall. TV rental. Play areas. Crèche. Bicycle hire. Cabins to rent. WiFi over part of site (charged). Off site: Golf 10 km. Boat launching 25 km.

Open: 30 March - 21 October.

Directions: Turn off Thisted-Fjerritslev 11 road to Klim from where site is signed.

GPS: 57.133333, 9.166667

Charges guide

Per unit incl. 2 persons and electricity	€ 31,00 - € 50,30
extra person	€ 11,00
child (1-11 yrs)	€ 8,20

Klim Strand Camping

Havvejen 167, Klim Strand, DK-9690 Fjerritslev (Nordjylland)
t: 98 22 53 40   e: ksc@klim-strand.dk
alanrogers.com/DK2170   www.klim-strand.dk

Accommodation: ⊘ Pitch ⊘ Mobile home/chalet ○ Hotel/B&B ○ Apartment

A large family holiday site right beside the sea, Klim Strand is a paradise for children. It is a privately owned TopCamp site with a full complement of quality facilities, including its own fire engine and trained staff. The site has 460 numbered touring pitches, all with electricity (10A), laid out in rows, many divided by trees and hedges, with shade in parts. Some 220 of these are extra large (180 sq.m) and fully serviced with electricity, water, drainage and TV hook-up. On-site activities include an outdoor water slide complex, an indoor pool, tennis courts and pony riding (all free). A wellness spa centre including a pirate-themed indoor play hall is a recent addition. For children there are numerous play areas, an adventure playground with aerial cable ride and a roller skating area. There is a kayak school and a large bouncy castle for toddlers. Live music and dancing are organised twice a week in high season. Suggested excursions include trips to offshore islands, visits to local potteries, a brewery museum and birdwatching on the Bygholm Vejle.

You might like to know

Fishing is popular here with all ages, either from the beach or on a boat trip out to sea.

- ⊘ Multi-lingual children's club – pre-school
- ⊘ Multi-lingual children's club – 5-10 year olds
- ⊘ Multi-lingual children's club – 10-14 year olds
- ⊘ Creative crafts
- ○ Bicycle hire for children
- ⊘ Facilities for children in the wash blocks
- ○ Children's pool
- ⊘ Children's play area
- ○ Crèche and/or babysitting
- ⊘ Local information of interest for children

Facilities: Sanitary facilities provide all the usual facilities plus some family bathrooms, special section for children, baby rooms and facilities for disabled campers. They could be stretched in high season. Basic wellness facility. Laundry. Motorcaravan services. Shop, bar/restaurant, pizzeria, takeaway (all open all season). Kitchen (water charged). Solarium. Indoor pool complex. Games and TV rooms. Indoor playroom for toddlers. Playground with moat. Animal farm. Internet access and WiFi (charged). Bicycle hire. Entertainment (main season). Boat launching with jetty. Communal barbecue.
Off site: Golf 10 km.

Open: 11 April - 19 October.

Directions: Site is on the coast midway between Nyborg and Svendborg. From 163 road just north of Hesselager, turn towards coast signed Bøsøre Strand (5 km).

GPS: 55.19287, 10.80530

Charges guide

Per unit incl. 2 persons and electricity	DKK 214 - 274
extra person	DKK 79
child (0-11 yrs)	DKK 53 - 70
dog	DKK 20

Bøsøre Strand Feriepark

Bøsørevej 16, DK-5874 Hesselager (Fyn)
t: 62 25 11 45 e: info@bosore.dk
alanrogers.com/DK2210 www.bosore.dk

Accommodation: ✔ Pitch ✔ Mobile home/chalet ◯ Hotel/B&B ◯ Apartment

A themed holiday site on the eastern coast of Fyn, the tales of Hans Christian Andersen are evident in the design of the indoor pool complex, the minigolf course and the main outdoor play area. The former has two pools on different levels, two hot tubs, a sauna and features characters from the stories; the latter has a fairytale castle with a moat as its centrepiece. There are 300 pitches in total (some up to 150 sq.m), and with only 25 seasonal units there should always be room for touring units out of the main season. All have 10A electricity, there are 124 multi-serviced pitches and 20 hardstandings. In common with several other sites in Denmark, Bøsøre operates a card system which allows use of the facilities (showers, sauna, solarium, washing machine etc). You only pay for what you have used when you leave. The card also operates the barriers and opens doors to other facilities.

You might like to know

The Tropical Water Park is constructed on three levels, with a sauna at the top from where you can enjoy views over the surrounding meadows where ponies graze. The upper pool is just 80 cm. deep and from there you can surf down into the big, 128 cm. deep pool.

- ✔ Multi-lingual children's club – pre-school
- ✔ Multi-lingual children's club – 5-10 year olds
- ◯ Multi-lingual children's club – 10-14 year olds
- ✔ Creative crafts
- ◯ Bicycle hire for children
- ✔ Facilities for children in the wash blocks
- ◯ Children's pool
- ✔ Children's play area
- ◯ Crèche and/or babysitting
- ✔ Local information of interest for children

45

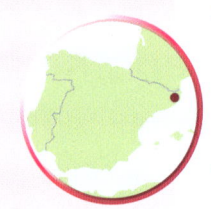

Kawan Village l'Amfora

Avenida Josep Tarradellas, 2, E-17470 Sant Pere Pescador (Girona)
t: 972 520 540 e: info@campingamfora.com
alanrogers.com/ES80350 www.campingamfora.com

Accommodation: ☑ Pitch ☑ Mobile home/chalet ○ Hotel/B&B ☑ Apartment

This spacious site is family run and friendly. It is spotlessly clean and well maintained and the owner operates in an environmentally friendly way. There are 830 level, grass pitches (741 for touring units) laid out in a grid system, all with 10A electricity. Attractive trees and shrubs have been planted around each pitch. There is good shade in the more mature areas, which include 64 large pitches (180 sq.m), each with an individual sanitary unit (toilet, shower and washbasin). The newer area is more open with less shade and you can choose which you would prefer. Three excellent sanitary blocks (one heated) are fully equipped and offer free hot water, each with staff on almost permanent duty to ensure very high standards. Access around the site is generally good for disabled visitors. At the entrance, which is hard surfaced with car parking, a terraced bar and two restaurants overlook a smart pool complex with three pools for children, one with two water slides. In high season (from July) there is ambitious evening entertainment (pub, disco, shows) and an activity programme for children.

You might like to know

Cots and high chairs are available to rent on site.

- ○ Multi-lingual children's club – pre-school
- ☑ Multi-lingual children's club – 5-10 year olds
- ☑ Multi-lingual children's club – 10-14 year olds
- ☑ Creative crafts
- ☑ Bicycle hire for children
- ☑ Facilities for children in the wash blocks
- ☑ Children's pool
- ☑ Children's play area
- ○ Crèche and/or babysitting
- ☑ Local information of interest for children

Facilities: Three main toilet blocks, one heated, provide washbasins in cabins and roomy free showers. Baby rooms. Laundry facilities and service. Motorcaravan services. Supermarket. Terraced bar, self-service and waiter-service restaurants. Pizzeria/takeaway. Restaurant and bar on the beach with limited menu (high season). Disco bar. Swimming pools (1/5-27/9). Pétanque. Tennis. Bicycle hire. Minigolf. Play area. Miniclub. Entertainment and activities. Windsurfing. Kite surfing (low season). Boat launching and sailing. Fishing. Exchange facilities. Games and TV rooms. Internet room and WiFi over site (charged). Car wash. Torches required in beach areas. Off site: Riding 4 km. Golf 15 km.

Open: 14 April - 27 September.

Directions: From north on A17/E15 take exit 3 on N11 towards Figueres and then shortly on C260 towards Roses. At Castello d'Empúries turn right on GIV6216 to Sant Pere. From south on A17 use exit 5 (L'Escala) and turn to Sant Pere in Viladamat. Site is well signed in town.

GPS: 42.18147, 3.10405

Charges guide

Per unit incl. 2 persons and electricity	€ 26,00 - € 60,00
extra person	€ 4,50 - € 6,20
child (2-9 yrs)	€ 2,50 - € 4,20
dog	€ 2,70 - € 5,20

Senior citizen specials. No credit cards.

Facilities: Five excellent large toilet blocks with electronic sliding glass doors (resident cleaners 07.00-21.00). British style toilets but no seats, controllable hot showers and washbasins in cabins. Excellent facilities for youngsters, babies and disabled campers. Laundry facilities. Motorcaravan services. Extensive supermarket, boutique and other shops. Large bar with terrace. Large restaurant. Takeaway and terrace. Ice cream parlour. Beach bar in main season. Disco club. Swimming pools. New adventure crazy golf. Playgrounds. Tennis. Archery (occasionally). Minigolf. Sailing/windsurfing school and other watersports. Programme of sports, games, excursions and entertainment, partly in English (15/6-31/8). Exchange facilities. ATM. Safety deposit. Internet café. WiFi over site (charged). Dogs taken in one section. Torches required in some areas. Off site: Resort of L'Escala 5 km. Riding and boat launching 5 km. Water park 10 km. Golf 30 km.

Open: 17 May - 19 September.

Directions: L'Escala is northeast of Girona on coast between Palamós and Roses. From A7/E15 autostrada take exit 5 towards L'Escala on GI623. Turn north 2 km. before L'Escala towards Sant Marti d'Ampúrias. Ths site is well signed.

GPS: 42.16098, 3.107774

Charges guide

Per unit incl. 2 persons and electricity	€ 22,50 - € 68,00
extra person	€ 3,50 - € 6,00
child (3-10 yrs)	€ 3,00 - € 3,50
dog	€ 3,20 - € 5,00

Camping Las Dunas

Ctra San Marti-Sant Pere, E-17470 Sant Pere Pescador (Girona)
t: 972 521 717   e: info@campinglasdunas.com
alanrogers.com/ES80400   www.campinglasdunas.com

Accommodation: ☑ Pitch   ☑ Mobile home/chalet   ○ Hotel/B&B   ○ Apartment

Las Dunas is an extremely large, impressive and well organised resort-style site with many on-site activities and an ongoing programme of improvements. It has direct access to a superb sandy beach that stretches along the site for nearly a kilometre with a windsurfing school and beach bar. There is also a much used, huge swimming pool, plus a large double pool for children. Las Dunas is very large, with 1,700 individual hedged pitches (1,500 for touring units) of around 100 sq.m. laid out on flat ground in long, regular parallel rows. All have electricity (6/10A) and 180 also have water and drainage. Shade is available in some parts of the site. Pitches are usually available, even in the main season. Much effort has gone into planting palms and new trees here and the results are very attractive. The large restaurant and bar have spacious terraces overlooking the swimming pools or you can enjoy a very pleasant, more secluded, cavern-style pub. A magnificent disco club is close by in a soundproofed building (although people returning from this during the night can be a problem for pitches in the central area of the site). A member of Leading Campings group.

You might like to know

Various sports competitions and games are organised by the campsite staff for both adults and children, and themed evenings introduce campers to flamenco, folk music and more.

- ○ Multi-lingual children's club – pre-school
- ☑ Multi-lingual children's club – 5-10 year olds
- ○ Multi-lingual children's club – 10-14 year olds
- ☑ Creative crafts
- ☑ Bicycle hire for children
- ☑ Facilities for children in the wash blocks
- ☑ Children's pool
- ☑ Children's play area
- ○ Crèche and/or babysitting
- ○ Local information of interest for children

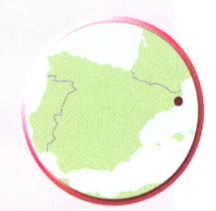

Facilities: Six excellent large and refurbished toilet blocks plus a seventh smaller block, all with resident cleaners, have showers using desalinated water and some washbasins in cabins. Facilities for disabled visitors. Laundry facilities. Motorcaravan services. Supermarket, shops, two restaurants, grills and pizzerias (all 28/4-23/9). Three bars. 'La Vela' barbecue and party area. Swimming pools with lifeguard (from 1/5). Large sports area. 2 km. exercise track. Dancing and entertainment weekly in season. Excursions and organised activities. Bicycle hire. Minigolf. Extensive new playground. Trampolines. Beach access. Scuba diving. Fishing. Hairdresser. ATM. Car servicing. Gas supplies. Internet café. WiFi over site (charged). Dogs are not accepted in high season (11/7-14/8). Off site: Golf (20% discount) and riding 4 km. Cycling and walking tracks.

Open: 28 April - 23 September.

Directions: From A7/E15 take exit 6 and C66 (Palafrugell). Then the GI642 east to Parlava and turn north on C31 (L'Escala). Cross River Ter and turn east on C31 (Ulla and Torroella de Montgri). Site signed off the C31 and has a long approach road. Watch for white dolphin marker and flags on the left.

GPS: 42.01197, 3.18807

Charges guide

Per unit incl. 2 persons and electricity	€ 22,75 - € 58,00
extra person	€ 4,75 - € 6,00
child (0-10 yrs)	€ 4,00 - € 5,00
dog (excl. 18/7-21/8)	€ 4,00 - € 5,00

Special offers on long stays in low season.

Camping El Delfin Verde

Ctra de Torroella de Montgrí, E-17257 Torroella de Montgrí (Girona)
t: 972 758 454   e: info@eldelfinverde.com
alanrogers.com/ES80800   www.eldelfinverde.com

Accommodation: ☑ Pitch   ☑ Mobile home/chalet   ○ Hotel/B&B   ☑ Apartment

A popular, self-contained and high quality site in a quiet location, El Delfin Verde has its own long beach stretching along its frontage, where activities such as scuba diving are organised. There is an attractive large pool in the shape of a dolphin with a total area of 1,800 sq.m. This is a large site with 917 touring pitches and around 6,000 visitors at peak times. It is well managed by friendly staff. Level grass pitches are 100-110 sq.m. and marked, with many separated by small fences and hedging. All have electricity (6A) and access to water points. There is shade in some of the older parts and a particularly pleasant area of pine trees in the centre provides marked but not separated pitches (sandy and not so level). Pitches by the beach lack shade. The pool has two island areas, one containing a huge fountain which can be lit at night. In the main season an elevated area with a large bar, restaurants and a separate takeaway gives wonderful views over the huge pool. One of the restaurants serves local dishes whilst the other has an international menu. There is also a takeaway, a pizzeria and a beach bar. There is an open-air arena for entertainment.

You might like to know

Children will enjoy the mini-disco with dancing, singing and games every evening in high season.

- ☑ Multi-lingual children's club – pre-school
- ☑ Multi-lingual children's club – 5-10 year olds
- ☑ Multi-lingual children's club – 10-14 year olds
- ☑ Creative crafts
- ○ Bicycle hire for children
- ☑ Facilities for children in the wash blocks
- ☑ Children's pool
- ☑ Children's play area
- ○ Crèche and/or babysitting
- ☑ Local information of interest for children

Facilities: Excellent toilet blocks can be heated and have controllable showers and many washbasins in cabins. Baby rooms. Units for disabled visitors. Serviced and self-service laundry. Motorcaravan services. Supermarket. Souvenir shop. Restaurants. Bar with simple meals and tapas. Outdoor pools (1/4-15/10), indoor pool (all year, charged). Wellness centre including sauna, jacuzzi and gym. Play areas. Sports field. Games room. Excursions. Activity and entertainment programme for all ages. Bicycle hire. Tennis. ATM and exchange facilities. WiFi throughout (charged). Caravan storage. Off site: Golf and riding 1 km. Fishing, sailing and boat launching 3 km. Shops, restaurants and bars in Vilanova 3 km. (local buses). Excursions arranged to Barcelona, Monserrat and Bodegas Torres (wine tasting).

Open: All year.

Directions: Site is 3 km. northwest of Vilanova i la Geltru towards L'Arboc (BV2115). From Tarragona on AP7 take exit 31 onto C32, then exit 16 for Vilanova. Site is on left in 2 km. From Barcelona take AP7 exit 29, C15 Vilanova, then C31 west to km. 153, and turn north on BV2115. Site is on right.

GPS: 41.23237, 1.69092

Charges guide

Per unit incl. 2 persons and electricity	€ 29,90 - € 51,50
extra person	€ 6,20 - € 11,10
child (4-11 yrs)	€ 3,60 - € 6,60
dog	€ 6,50 - € 13,20

No credit cards.

Vilanova Park

Ctra de l'Arboc km. 2.5, E-08800 Vilanova i la Geltru (Barcelona)
t: 938 933 402   e: info@vilanovapark.com
alanrogers.com/ES83900   www.vilanovapark.com

Accommodation: ☑ Pitch   ☑ Mobile home/chalet   ○ Hotel/B&B   ○ Apartment

Sitting on the terrace in front of the restaurant – a beautifully converted Catalan farmhouse dating from 1908 – it is difficult to believe that in 1982 this was still a farm with few trees and known as Mas Roque (Rock Farm). Since then, imaginative planting has led to there being literally thousands of trees and gloriously colourful shrubs making this large campsite most attractive. It has an impressive range of high quality amenities and facilities open all year. There are 343 marked pitches for touring units in separate areas, all with electricity 6/10A, 168 larger pitches also have water and, in some cases, drainage. They are on hard surfaces, on gently sloping ground and with plenty of shade. A further 1,000 or so pitches are mostly occupied by chalets to rent, and by tour operators. The amenities include an excellent pool with water jets and at night time a coloured, floodlit fountain, which complements the dancing and entertainment taking place in the courtyard above. Nearby is a pleasant nature park with picnic tables. A second pool higher up the site has marvellous views across the town to the sea.

You might like to know

Families will have hours of fun on the minigolf course, and there is a jumping pillow – a trampoline with a difference!

○ Multi-lingual children's club – pre-school
☑ Multi-lingual children's club – 5-10 year olds
☑ Multi-lingual children's club – 10-14 year olds
☑ Creative crafts
○ Bicycle hire for children
☑ Facilities for children in the wash blocks
☑ Children's pool
☑ Children's play area
○ Crèche and/or babysitting
☑ Local information of interest for children

Facilities: The six sanitary blocks are constantly cleaned and are always exceptional, including many individual cabins with en suite facilities. Improvements are made each year. Some blocks have excellent facilities for babies. Launderette with service. Motorcaravan services. Car wash (charged). Gas supplies. Snack bars. Indoor and outdoor restaurants with takeaway. Swimming pools. Fitness centre. Sports complex. Fitness room (charged). Playgrounds including adventure play area. Miniclub. Minigolf. Multiple Internet options including WiFi (free). Security bracelets. Medical centre. Off site: Beach activities 50 m. Bus at gate. Bicycle hire 100 m. Fishing 200 m. Riding 3 km. Port Aventura 4 km. Aquopolis and golf 5 km.

Open: 20 March - 2 November.

Directions: On west side of Salou 1 km. from the centre, site is well signed from the coast road to Cambrils and from the other town approaches.

GPS: 41.07546, 1.11651

Charges guide

Per unit incl. 2 persons
and electricity € 29,00 - € 78,00

extra person € 7,00

child (4-12 yrs) € 5,00

Reductions outside high season for longer stays. Special long stay offers for senior citizens.

Camping Resort Sanguli Salou

Passeig Miramar-Plaça Venus, Apdo 123, E-43840 Salou (Tarragona)
t: 977 381 641 e: mail@sanguli.es
alanrogers.com/ES84800 www.sanguli.es

Accommodation: ☑ Pitch ☑ Mobile home/chalet ◯ Hotel/B&B ◯ Apartment

Camping Resort Sanguli Salou is a superb site boasting excellent pools and entertainment. Owned, developed and managed by a local Spanish family, it has something for all the family with everything open when the site is open. There are 1,089 pitches of varying sizes (75-120 sq.m) all with electricity (7.5/10A). Mobile homes occupy 58 pitches and there are fully equipped bungalows on 147. A wonderful selection of trees, palms and shrubs provide natural shade and an ideal space for children to play. The good sandy beach is little more than 50 metres across the coast road and a small railway crossing. Although large, Sanguli has a pleasant, open feel and maintains a quality family atmosphere due to the efforts of the very keen and efficient staff. There are three very attractive themed pools, which include water slides and elephants. Amenities include a children's play park, organised activities for adults and children, a miniclub, tennis courts, table tennis, minigolf, a football pitch, volleyball, and a fitness room. Evening shows are presented in the site's magnificent amphitheatre, there is a cinema and the Sanguli restaurant serves Mediterranean cuisine.

You might like to know

Special services for children include a miniclub with its mascot, Guli, sports competitions and childrens shows. Loan of cots. Children's menu, high chairs and bibs in the restaurant.

◯ Multi-lingual children's club – pre-school
☑ Multi-lingual children's club – 5-10 year olds
☑ Multi-lingual children's club – 10-14 year olds
☑ Creative crafts
◯ Bicycle hire for children
☑ Facilities for children in the wash blocks
☑ Children's pool
☑ Children's play area
◯ Crèche and/or babysitting
☑ Local information of interest for children

Facilities: Very good quality sanitary buildings with washbasins in private cabins and separate WCs. Facilities for babies and disabled campers. Several launderettes. Motorcaravan services. Gas. Good shopping centre. Restaurants and bars. Fitness suite. Hairdresser. TV lounges. Beach bar. Playground. Jogging track. Sports area. Tennis. Minigolf. Organised activities including pottery. Pedalo hire. Boat mooring. Bicycle hire. Internet café. WiFi over site (charged). Dogs are not accepted. Off site: Public transport 100 m. from gate. Riding, golf and boat launching 3 km.

Open: 4 April - 26 October.

Directions: Site entrance is off main N340 nearly 30 km. southwest from Tarragona. From motorway take Cambrils exit and turn west on N340 at 1136 km. marker.

GPS: 41.03345, 0.96921

Charges guide

Per unit incl. 2 persons
and electricity € 19,00 - € 56,00

extra person € 6,50 - € 8,00

child (3-10 yrs) no charge - € 6,00

Discounts for longer stays and for pensioners.

Spain – Montroig

Playa Montroig Camping Resort

Ctra N340 km. 1136, E-43300 Montroig (Tarragona)
t: 977 810 637   e: info@playamontroig.com
alanrogers.com/ES85300   www.playamontroig.com

Accommodation: ☑ Pitch   ☑ Mobile home/chalet   ○ Hotel/B&B   ○ Apartment

What a superb site! Playa Montroig is about 30 kilometres beyond Tarragona set in its own tropical gardens with direct access to a very long, narrow, soft sand beach. The main part of the site lies between the sea, road and railway (as at other sites on this coast, there is some train noise) with a huge underpass. The site is divided into spacious, marked pitches with excellent shade provided by a variety of lush vegetation including very impressive palms set in wide avenues. There are 1,050 pitches, all with electricity (10A) and 564 with water and drainage. Some 47 pitches are directly alongside the beach. The site has many outstanding features: there is an excellent pool complex near the entrance, with two pools (one heated). A new Espai Grill and bar with a rock and roll disco and a pretty candlelit patio is just outside the gate. One restaurant (seating 150) serves good food with some Catalan fare and overlooks an entertainment area. A member of Leading Campings group.

You might like to know

The entertainment team organises numerous parties, events, competitions, courses and much more. And there's special emphasis on children – they have their own clubs, play areas, parties and shows, all providing special memories of their holiday.

- ☑ Multi-lingual children's club – pre-school
- ☑ Multi-lingual children's club – 5-10 year olds
- ☑ Multi-lingual children's club – 10-14 year olds
- ☑ Creative crafts
- ○ Bicycle hire for children
- ☑ Facilities for children in the wash blocks
- ☑ Children's pool
- ☑ Children's play area
- ○ Crèche and/or babysitting
- ☑ Local information of interest for children

Facilities: The elegant sanitary blocks offer the very best of modern facilities and are regularly cleaned. Heated in winter, they include private cabins and facilities for disabled visitors and babies. Laundry facilities. Motorcaravan services. Gas. Supermarket. Bars. Restaurant and café. Ice-cream kiosk. Swimming pools (1/4-15/10). Indoor pool. Fitness centre. Sauna. Solarium. Jacuzzi. Play rooms. Extensive activity and entertainment programme including barbecues and swimming nights. Sports area. Tennis. Huge playgrounds. Hairdresser. Bicycle hire. Road train to beach. Exclusive area for dogs. Internet café (charged) and free WiFi. Off site: Fishing 700 m. Boat launching 5 km. Golf 7 km. Riding 15 km. Hourly bus service from outside the gate. Theme parks.

Open: All year.

Directions: Site is 2 km. west of La Marina. Leave N332 Guardamara de Segura-Santa Pola road at 75 km. marker if travelling north, or 78 km. marker if travelling south. Site is well signed.

GPS: 38.129649, -0.649575

Charges guide

Per unit incl. 2 persons and all services	€ 31,00 - € 49,00
extra person	€ 6,00 - € 8,50
child (3-10 yrs)	€ 4,50 - € 6,00
dog	€ 1,10 - € 2,50

Good discounts for longer stays in low season.

Spain – La Marina

Camping Internacional La Marina

Ctra N332 km. 76, E-03194 La Marina (Alacant)
t: 965 419 200 e: info@campinglamarina.com
alanrogers.com/ES87420 www.campinglamarina.com

Accommodation: ☑ Pitch ☑ Mobile home/chalet ○ Hotel/B&B ○ Apartment

Very efficiently run by a friendly Belgian family, La Marina has 465 touring pitches of three different types and sizes ranging from 50 sq.m. to 150 sq.m. with electricity (10/16A), TV, water and drainage. Artificial shade is provided and the pitches are extremely well maintained on level, well drained ground with a special area allocated for tents in a small orchard. The huge lagoon swimming pool complex is absolutely fabulous and has something for everyone (with lifeguards). William Le Metayer, the owner, is passionate about La Marina and it shows in his search for perfection. A magnificent new, modern building which uses the latest architectural technology, houses many superb extra amenities. Facilities include a relaxed business centre with Internet access, a tapas bar decorated with amazing ceramics (handmade by the owner's mother) and a quality restaurant with a water fountain feature and great views of the lagoon. There is also a conference centre and a large computerised library. A member of Leading Campings group.

You might like to know

There is a wide range of programmed activities for children, adults and teenagers, including shows, competitions, workshops, cookery classes, Spanish courses and much more.

- ☑ Multi-lingual children's club – pre-school
- ☑ Multi-lingual children's club – 5-10 year olds
- ☑ Multi-lingual children's club – 10-14 year olds
- ☑ Creative crafts
- ☑ Bicycle hire for children
- ☑ Facilities for children in the wash blocks
- ☑ Children's pool
- ☑ Children's play area
- ○ Crèche and/or babysitting
- ☑ Local information of interest for children

Facilities: Six excellent, spacious and fully equipped toilet blocks include baby baths. Large laundry. Motorcaravan services. Gas supplies. Freezer service. Supermarket. General shop. Kiosk. Restaurant and bar. Takeaway (July/Aug). Swimming pools, bathing caps compulsory (20/5-15/9). Entertainment organised with a soundproofed pub/disco (July/Aug). Gym park. Tennis. Playground. Riding. Fishing. Nature animal park. Hairdresser (July/Aug). Medical centre. Torches necessary in some areas. Animals are not accepted. WiFi on part of site (charged). Off site: Bicycle hire and large sports complex with multiple facilities including an indoor pool 1 km. Sailing and boat launching 10 km. Riding and golf 20 km.

Open: 27 March - 27 September.

Directions: From A8 (Bilbao-Santander) take km. 185 exit and N634 towards Beranga. Almost immediately turn right on CA147 to Noja. In 10 km. turn left at multiple campsite signs and go through town. At beach follow signs to site.

GPS: 43.48948, -3.53700

Charges guide

Per unit incl. 2 persons and electricity	€ 28,90 - € 49,20
extra person	€ 4,50 - € 7,00
child (3-9 yrs)	€ 3,15 - € 5,10

Low season discounts.

Spain – Noja

Camping Playa Joyel

Playa de Ris, E-39180 Noja (Cantabria)
t: 942 630 081   e: info@playjoyel.com
alanrogers.com/ES90000   www.playajoyel.com

Accommodation: ✔ Pitch   ✔ Mobile home/chalet   ○ Hotel/B&B   ○ Apartment

This very attractive holiday and touring site is some 40 kilometres from Santander and 80 kilometres from Bilbao. It is a busy, high quality, comprehensively equipped site by a superb beach providing 1,000 well shaded, marked and numbered pitches with 6A electricity available. These include 80 large pitches of 100 sq.m. Some 250 pitches are occupied by tour operators and seasonal units. This well managed site has a lot to offer for family holidays with much going on in high season when it gets crowded. The swimming pool complex (with lifeguard) is free to campers and the superb beaches are cleaned daily mid-June to mid-September. Two beach exits lead to the main beach where there are some undertows, or if you turn left you will find a reasonably placid estuary. An unusual feature here is the nature park within the site boundary which has a selection of animals to see. This overlooks a protected area of marsh where European birds spend the winter.

You might like to know

Why not visit Santillana del Mar, a beautiful old town with winding medieval streets.

- ✔ Multi-lingual children's club – pre-school
- ✔ Multi-lingual children's club – 5-10 year olds
- ✔ Multi-lingual children's club – 10-14 year olds
- ✔ Creative crafts
- ○ Bicycle hire for children
- ✔ Facilities for children in the wash blocks
- ✔ Children's pool
- ✔ Children's play area
- ○ Crèche and/or babysitting
- ○ Local information of interest for children

Facilities: Three toilet blocks, only two open in low season. Excellent children's area in the main block. Facilities for disabled visitors. Motorcaravan services. Bar (all season) and restaurant/pizzeria (1/5-15/9). Outdoor swimming pool (1/5-26/9) and covered heated pool. Boules. Play area. Trampoline. Multisports court. Miniclub (mainly 6-12 yrs; 1/5-11/9). Entertainment (high season). WiFi at the bar (free). Only gas barbecues are permitted. Chalets, mobile homes and tents for rent. Off site: Supermarket 100 m. Bicycle hire 2 km. Riding 5 km.

Open: 11 April - 26 September.

Directions: From the A7 motorway (Loriol) take exit 16 towards Privas. At Le Pouzin use heavy goods route, D86, D22 then D2. In Privas at roundabout (near Intermarché) look for signs Espace Ouvéze exit left and take second left, signed campsite and Espace Ouvéze.

GPS: 44.72611, 4.59845

Charges guide

Per unit incl. 2 persons and electricity	€ 21,00 - € 32,00
extra person	€ 6,00 - € 8,40
child (3-12 yrs)	€ 3,00 - € 6,80
dog	€ 3,50

Kawan Village Ardèche Camping

Boulevard de Paste, F-07000 Privas (Ardèche)
t: 04 75 64 05 80   e: jcray@wanadoo.fr
alanrogers.com/FR07180   www.ardechecamping.fr

Accommodation: ☑ Pitch   ☑ Mobile home/chalet   ○ Hotel/B&B   ○ Apartment

This spacious, family run site is on the southern outskirts of Privas and aims to provide a warm and friendly atmosphere. The site has 166 large, grass, mostly level pitches, of which 112 are for touring units with 10A electricity and trees offering varying degrees of shade. It is a comfortable base for exploring the lesser known parts of the Ardèche with bus and coach trips available. On site there is something for all ages with a bar, restaurant, heated swimming pool complex, and a multisports area with outdoor gym equipment. A welcome drink is offered each Sunday evening, when details of the attractions in the area are given. The campsite has a mascot which helps make the miniclub more special. A variety of activities is on offer for children aged five years and over, supervised by French, English and Dutch speaking leaders. There is a children's disco party evening once a week. The campsite is a good base for day trips to the region which features the Ardèche river with canyoning, canoeing, climbing and potholing. For the less adventurous there are caves and a number of France's best villages with character and charm to visit.

You might like to know

Children over 5 years are supervised by multi-lingual staff (Monday to Saturday mornings), while they enjoy creative play, outdoor games and tucking into crêpes in the company of Kawan, the site mascot.

- ○ Multi-lingual children's club – pre-school
- ☑ Multi-lingual children's club – 5-10 year olds
- ☑ Multi-lingual children's club – 10-14 year olds
- ☑ Creative crafts
- ○ Bicycle hire for children
- ☑ Facilities for children in the wash blocks
- ☑ Children's pool
- ☑ Children's play area
- ○ Crèche and/or babysitting
- ☑ Local information of interest for children

Kawan Village les Genêts

Lac de Pareloup, F-12410 Salles-Curan (Aveyron)
t: 05 65 46 35 34 e: contact@camping-les-genets.fr
alanrogers.com/FR12080 www.camping-les-genets.fr

Accommodation: ☑ Pitch ☑ Mobile home/chalet ○ Hotel/B&B ○ Apartment

This family run site is on the shores of Lac de Pareloup and offers both family holiday and watersports facilities. The 163 pitches include 80 grassy, mostly individual pitches for touring units. These are in two areas, one on each side of the entrance lane, and are divided by hedges, shrubs and trees. All have electricity (6A) and many also have water and waste water drain. The site slopes gently down to the beach and lake with facilities for all watersports including water-skiing. A full entertainment and activities programme is organised in high season, and there is much to see and do in this very attractive corner of Aveyron. Used by tour operators (25 pitches). The site is not suitable for American-style motorhomes.

You might like to know

There is plenty to keep children busy – a heated swimming pool, a water trampoline, a moonwalk on the lake and a disco for teenagers. In July and August, there is entertainment for the over 4s.

- ☑ Multi-lingual children's club – pre-school
- ☑ Multi-lingual children's club – 5-10 year olds
- ☑ Multi-lingual children's club – 10-14 year olds
- ☑ Creative crafts
- ☑ Bicycle hire for children
- ☑ Facilities for children in the wash blocks
- ☑ Children's pool
- ☑ Children's play area
- ○ Crèche and/or babysitting
- ☑ Local information of interest for children

Facilities: Two sanitary units, one refurbished, with suite for disabled guests. Baby room. Laundry. Well stocked shop and heated outdoor pool (1/6-14/9). Bar (1/6-7/9). Restaurant and takeaway (23/6-7/9). Play area. Minigolf. Boules. Bicycle hire. Pedalos, windsurfers, kayaks. WiFi throughout (free). Off site: Riding 6 km. Medieval village of Castelnau Pegayrolles. Canyoning and many walking routes. Millau for its shopping and spectacular bridge over the Tarn river. Guided tours of Roquefort cheesemakers.

Open: 17 May - 14 September.

Directions: From Salles-Curan take D577 for 4 km. and turn right into a narrow lane immediately after a sharp right-hand bend. Site is signed at junction.

GPS: 44.18933, 2.76693

Charges guide

Per unit incl. 2 persons and electricity	€ 18,00 - € 41,00
extra person	€ 4,00 - € 8,00
child (2-7 yrs)	no charge - € 7,00
dog	€ 3,00 - € 4,00

Facilities: Modern toilet blocks have all the necessary facilities including those for disabled visitors. Shop. Bar. Restaurant, takeaway (reduced opening in low season). Swimming pool complex. Large play area. Boules. Tennis. Football. Organised activities (July/Aug). Fishing. Bicycle hire (July/Aug). Motorboat launching. Watersports (July/Aug). Swimming in lake. Max. 2 dogs (1 in rentals). WiFi (charged). Off site: Paths by lake. Other marked walks and cycle rides. Shops, banks, restaurants 8 km. Riding 13 km. Golf 30 km. Canoeing, rafting, paragliding and windsurfing.

Open: 11 May - 5 September.

Directions: From D911 Rodez-Millau road, just east of Pont de Salars, turn south on D993 signed Salles-Curan. In 6 km. at crossroads turn right on D538 signed le Caussanel. Very shortly turn left and continue to site.

GPS: 44.21462, 2.76658

Charges guide

Per unit incl. 2 persons and electricity € 18,80 - € 35,35	
extra person € 4,40 - € 7,70	
child (2-6 yrs) € 3,10 - € 5,30	
dog € 3,90	

France – Canet-de-Salars

Castels Camping le Caussanel

Lac de Pareloup, F-12290 Canet-de-Salars (Aveyron)
t: 05 65 46 85 19 e: info@lecaussanel.com
alanrogers.com/FR12170 www.lecaussanel.com

Accommodation: ☑ Pitch ☑ Mobile home/chalet ○ Hotel/B&B ○ Apartment

This is an attractive site with amenities for all the family. It has 228 large, fairly level, grassy pitches, 108 for touring. Most have some shade, 6A electricity (very long leads may be necessary), and 45 are fully serviced. The pitches are defined by lines and offer little privacy but some have wonderful views over the lake. The site has swimming pools with toboggan and slides and a large paddling pool for children, with small slides. The adjacent 1,200-hectare lake offers a large area for swimming and all the usual watersports. This large, extremely spacious site on the banks of Lac de Pareloup is greatly improved. It is ideal in low season for those seeking a tranquil holiday in a beautiful region of France, or in high season for those seeking an active holiday.

You might like to know

The kids will love the animal farm in July and August. There is a miniclub for children aged 4-10 years, and a youth club for youngsters aged 11-17 years.

○ Multi-lingual children's club – pre-school
☑ Multi-lingual children's club – 5-10 year olds
☑ Multi-lingual children's club – 10-14 year olds
☑ Creative crafts
☑ Bicycle hire for children
○ Facilities for children in the wash blocks
☑ Children's pool
☑ Children's play area
○ Crèche and/or babysitting
☑ Local information of interest for children

Facilities: Three spotlessly clean luxurious toilet blocks (one heated) include units with washbasin and shower and facilities for disabled visitors and children. Large laundry. Motorcaravan services. Gas supplies. Large supermarket. Boutique. Restaurant/bar and takeaway. Impressive swimming pool complex with water slides and large paddling pool. Massage (July/Aug). Multisports pitch. Tennis. Games and TV rooms. Bicycle hire. Updated play areas. Organised entertainment/excursions in high season. Clubs for children all season. Pony trekking. Children's farm. WiFi (charged). Off site: Supermarket and bank 5 km. Fishing 5 km. Golf 15 km. Flying trips. Ile d'Oléron. La Rochelle.

Open: 16 May - 13 September.

Directions: Site is 5 km. southeast of Marennes. From Rochefort take D733 south for 12 km. Turn west on D123 to Ile d'Oléron. Continue for 12 km. Turn southeast on D728 (Saintes). Site signed, in 1 km. on left. From A10 at Saintes take D728 and turn right shortly after St Just. Site signed.

GPS: 45.81095, -1.06109

Charges guide

Per unit incl. 2 persons and electricity	€ 21,00 - € 55,00
extra person	€ 7,00 - € 10,00
child (3-9 yrs)	€ 3,00 - € 6,00
dog	€ 5,00

Castel Camping Séquoia Parc

La Josephtrie, F-17320 Saint Just-Luzac (Charente-Maritime)
t: 05 46 85 55 55   e: info@sequoiaparc.com
alanrogers.com/FR17140   www.sequoiaparc.com

Accommodation: ☑ Pitch   ☑ Mobile home/chalet   ○ Hotel/B&B   ○ Apartment

This is definitely a site not to be missed. Approached by an avenue of flowers, shrubs and trees, Séquoia Parc is a Castel site set in the grounds of La Josephtrie, a striking château with beautifully restored outbuildings and courtyard area with a bar and restaurant. Most of the 640 pitches are about 140 sq.m. with 6/10A electricity connections and separated by mature shrubs providing plenty of privacy. The site has 350 mobile homes and chalets, with a further 65 used by tour operators. This is a popular site and reservation is necessary in high season. Children's clubs are run all season (4-7 yrs and 7-12 yrs), with entertainment provided in high season. The site itself is designed to a high specification with reception in a large, light and airy room retaining its original beams and leading to the courtyard area where you find the bar and restaurant. The pool complex with water slides, large paddling pool and sunbathing area is impressive. A new terraced area adjacent to the snack bar allows you to enjoy your food in a very pleasant garden setting with sunshades. A member of Leading Campings group.

You might like to know

This is an ideal site to discover horse riding. There are eight very friendly ponies to help your child gain confidence, plus horses to suit different levels.

- ○ Multi-lingual children's club – pre-school
- ☑ Multi-lingual children's club – 5-10 year olds
- ☑ Multi-lingual children's club – 10-14 year olds
- ☑ Creative crafts
- ☑ Bicycle hire for children
- ☑ Facilities for children in the wash blocks
- ☑ Children's pool
- ☑ Children's play area
- ○ Crèche and/or babysitting
- ☑ Local information of interest for children

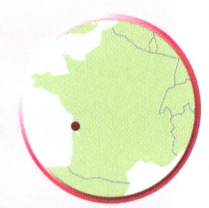

Facilities

Facilities: Three clean, unheated sanitary blocks have spacious, well equipped showers and washbasins (mainly in cabins). Baby facilities. Excellent facilities for disabled visitors. Private facilities (shower, basin and toilet) to rent. Laundry rooms. Motorcaravan services. Superb restaurant/takeaway and bar (July/Aug). Shop (July/Aug). Heated indoor swimming pool (all season). Jacuzzi. Sauna. Playground. Games room. Football field. Tennis. Minigolf. Fishing. Archery (high season). Bicycle hire. Canoe hire. Free WiFi on part of site. No charcoal barbecues. Kids' club. Lending library. Off site: Beach 300 m. Supermarket 2 km. Sailing 2 km. Riding 6 km. Golf 7 km.

Open: 28 March - 8 November.

Directions: After crossing bridge to l'Ile d'Oléron turn right towards Château d'Oléron. Continue through village and follow sign for Route des Huitres. Site is on left after 2.5 km.

GPS: 45.90415, -1.21525

Charges guide

Per unit incl. 2 persons and electricity	€ 21,90 - € 44,00
extra person	€ 5,50 - € 8,50
dog	€ 3,50

France – Le Château-d'Oléron

Camping la Brande

Route des Huitres, F-17480 Le Château-d'Oléron (Charente-Maritime)
t: 05 46 47 62 37 e: info@camping-labrande.com
alanrogers.com/FR17220 www.camping-labrande.com

Accommodation: ☑ Pitch ☑ Mobile home/chalet ○ Hotel/B&B ○ Apartment

An environmentally friendly site, run and maintained to a high standard, la Brande offers an ideal holiday environment on the delightful Ile d'Oléron. It is situated on the oyster route and close to a sandy beach. Pitches here are generous and mostly separated by hedges and trees, the greater number for touring outfits. All are on level grassy terrain and have electricity hook-ups, some are fully serviced. Some of the most attractive pitches are in a newer section towards the back of the site. The many activities during the high season, plus the natural surroundings, make this an ideal choice for families. A feature of this site is the heated indoor pool (28ºC) open all season. The Barcat family ensures that their visitors not only enjoy quality facilities, but Gerard Barcat offers guided bicycle tours and canoe trips. This way you discover the nature, oyster farming, vineyards and history of Oléron, which is joined to the mainland by a 3 km. bridge.

You might like to know

The children's club, P'tits Loubinats, welcomes your children (5-12 yrs) throughout July and August with a varied activity and entertainment programme, supervised by a qualified, English-speaking team.

- ☑ Multi-lingual children's club – pre-school
- ☑ Multi-lingual children's club – 5-10 year olds
- ☑ Multi-lingual children's club – 10-14 year olds
- ☑ Creative crafts
- ☑ Bicycle hire for children
- ☑ Facilities for children in the wash blocks
- ☑ Children's pool
- ☑ Children's play area
- ○ Crèche and/or babysitting
- ☑ Local information of interest for children

Facilities: Heated sanitary block with facilities for children and disabled visitors. Laundry room. Shop, bar, restaurant and takeaway (all season). Swimming pool complex with flumes and toboggan (15/5-10/9). Large indoor pool complex with spa and toboggan. Massage room. Wellness centre. Games room. Family entertainment programme. Multisports court. Aerial zip wire course. Climbing wall. Bicycle hire. WiFi over site (charged). Dogs accepted all season except in 4-star and premium accommodation. Off site: Bénodet 1 km. Beach and fishing 1 km. Riding 2 km. Golf 3 km.

Open: 3 April - 13 September.

Directions: Take the D34 south from Quimper. Site is on the left just as you enter Bénodet.

GPS: 47.882065, -4.103282

Charges guide

Contact the site for details.

France – Bénodet

Yelloh! Village Port de Plaisance

Lieu-dit Prad Poullou, B.P. 46, Clohars Fouesnant, F-29950 Bénodet (Finistère)
t: 02 98 57 02 38 e: info@campingbenodet.fr
alanrogers.com/FR29380 www.campingbenodet.fr

Accommodation: ○ Pitch ☑ Mobile home/chalet ○ Hotel/B&B ○ Apartment

Sometimes larger campsites can lack ambiance, but it is not so with Port de Plaisance. This site has 353 pitches, all of which are occupied by accommodation to rent. There are no touring pitches here. Accommodation is mostly in two areas, positioned in small groups amongst the many mature trees and flowering shrubs. Although there are five holiday tour operators on site, their presence is unobtrusive because of careful positioning amongst the trees. A wide range of entertainment and activities take place over a long season, and the large indoor water complex is impressive. The restaurant that overlooks the pool complex boasts a very good menu. There is entertainment suitable for all ages. Covered heated pool. The marina at the mouth of the Odet river is 500 m. away, and from here you can enjoy a boat trip up to Quimper. The large seaside town of Bénodet, with all the shops, bars and restaurants that you could wish for is just 1 km. away.

You might like to know

Activities include an adventure course in the trees, trampolines and a rock climbing wall.

○ Multi-lingual children's club – pre-school
☑ Multi-lingual children's club – 5-10 year olds
☑ Multi-lingual children's club – 10-14 year olds
☑ Creative crafts
☑ Bicycle hire for children
☑ Facilities for children in the wash blocks
☑ Children's pool
☑ Children's play area
○ Crèche and/or babysitting
☑ Local information of interest for children

Le Camp de Florence

Route Astaffort, F-32480 La Romieu (Gers)
t: 05 62 28 15 58 e: info@lecampdeflorence.com
alanrogers.com/FR32010 www.lecampdeflorence.com

Accommodation: ☑ Pitch ☑ Mobile home/chalet ○ Hotel/B&B ○ Apartment

Camp de Florence is an attractive and very well equipped site on the edge of an historic village in pleasantly undulating Gers countryside. The 197 large, part terraced pitches (100 for touring units) all have 10A electricity, 20 with hardstanding and 16 fully serviced. They are arranged around a large field with rural views, giving a feeling of spaciousness. The 13th-century village of La Romieu is on the Santiago de Compostela pilgrims' route. The Pyrenees are a two hour drive, the Atlantic coast a similar distance. The site has been developed by the friendly Mijnsbergen family. They have sympathetically converted the old farmhouse buildings to provide facilities for the site. The Collegiate church, a UNESCO World Heritage monument, is visible from the site and well worth visiting (the views from the top of the tower are magnificent). The local arboretum has the biggest collection of trees in the Midi-Pyrénées.

You might like to know

There is a children's club six days a week in July and August. Popular activities include a treasure hunt, an evening swim with music and dancing, and a pancake party.

○ Multi-lingual children's club – pre-school
☑ Multi-lingual children's club – 5-10 year olds
☑ Multi-lingual children's club – 10-14 year olds
☑ Creative crafts
☑ Bicycle hire for children
☑ Facilities for children in the wash blocks
☑ Children's pool
☑ Children's play area
○ Crèche and/or babysitting
☑ Local information of interest for children

Facilities: Three toilet blocks provide all the necessary facilities. Washing machines and dryers. Motorcaravan services. Restaurant (1/5-30/9, also open to the public). Takeaway. Bread. Swimming pool area with water slide. Jacuzzi. Protected children's pool (open to public in afternoons). New playgrounds, games and animal park. Bouncy castle. Trampoline. Outdoor fitness machines. Games room. Tennis. Pétanque. Bicycle hire. Discos, picnics, musical evenings. WiFi over site (charged, free in bar). Max. 2 dogs. Off site: Shop 500 m. in village. Fishing 5 km. Riding 10 km. Walking tours. Walibi theme park nearby.

Open: 1 April - 10 October.

Directions: Site signed from D931 Agen-Condom road. Small units turn left at Ligardes (signed), follow D36 for 1 km, turn right at La Romieu (signed). Otherwise continue to outskirts of Condom and take D41 left to La Romieu, through village to site.
GPS: 43.98299, 0.50183

Charges guide

Per unit incl. 2 persons and electricity	€ 17,00 - € 41,00
extra person	€ 3,90 - € 8,00
child (4-17 yrs)	no charge - € 7,60
dog (max. 2)	€ 2,00 - € 3,00

Facilities: Very clean sanitary blocks include provision for disabled visitors. Washing machines. Motorcaravan services. Large supermarket, restaurant, takeaway, pizzeria and bar. Four outdoor pools with slides and flumes (20/5-10/9). Indoor pool (all season). Fitness room. Massage (Institut de Beauté). Tennis. Play areas. Miniclub, organised entertainment in season. Bicycle hire. WiFi throughout site (charged). ATM. Charcoal barbecues are not permitted. Hotel (12 rooms). Off site: Path to the beach 300 m. Fishing and riding. Golf 30 km.

Open: 13 May - 13 September.

Directions: Turn off D101 Hourtin-Soulac road 3 km. north of Hourtin. Then join D101E signed Hourtin-Plage. Site is 300 m. from the beach.

GPS: 45.22297, -1.16465

Charges guide

Per unit incl. 2 persons
and electricity € 30,00 - € 58,00

extra person € 5,00 - € 10,00

child (3-9 yrs) € 4,00 - € 9,00

dog € 3,00 - € 7,00

France – Hourtin-Plage

Airotel Camping de la Côte d'Argent

F-33990 Hourtin-Plage (Gironde)
t: 05 56 09 10 25 e: info@cca33.com
alanrogers.com/FR33110 www.cca33.com

Accommodation: ☑ Pitch ☑ Mobile home/chalet ☑ Hotel/B&B ○ Apartment

Côte d'Argent is a large, well equipped site for leisurely family holidays. It makes an ideal base for walkers and cyclists with over 100 km. of cycle lanes in the area. Hourtin-Plage is a pleasant invigorating resort on the Atlantic coast and a popular location for watersports enthusiasts. The site's top attraction is its pool complex, where wooden bridges connect the pools and islands, and there are sunbathing and play areas plus an indoor heated pool. The site has 600 touring pitches (all with 10A electricity), not always clearly defined, arranged under trees with some on sand. High quality entertainment takes place at the impressive bar/restaurant near the entrance. Spread over 20 hectares of undulating sand-based terrain and in the midst of a pine forest, the site is well organised and ideal for children.

You might like to know

A mini-club for children aged 6-11 years runs during the whole of July and August.

- ○ Multi-lingual children's club – pre-school
- ☑ Multi-lingual children's club – 5-10 year olds
- ○ Multi-lingual children's club – 10-14 year olds
- ☑ Creative crafts
- ○ Bicycle hire for children
- ☑ Facilities for children in the wash blocks
- ☑ Children's pool
- ☑ Children's play area
- ○ Crèche and/or babysitting
- ○ Local information of interest for children

Yelloh! Village Club Farret

Chemin des Rosses, F-34450 Vias-Plage (Hérault)
t: 04 67 21 64 45   e: farret@wanadoo.fr
alanrogers.com/FR34110   www.yellohvillage.co.uk/camping/le_club_farret

Accommodation: ✓ Pitch   ✓ Mobile home/chalet   ○ Hotel/B&B   ○ Apartment

An excellent site for families, well maintained and attractively landscaped with flowering shrubs, giving a truly Mediterranean feel. The main area has beach frontage and touring pitches, the other half, across a lane, has high quality mobile homes. Staff are helpful and everywhere is neat and tidy. It is a large, busy site but well organised with a relaxed atmosphere. There are 756 good sized, level, grassy pitches, with 302 for touring (10A electricity) with some shade from many trees. Both areas have impressive pool complexes, the newest has a pool bar. The safe beach is alongside the site, so some pitches have sea views as does the restaurant high above the pool. Evening entertainment and cultural visits are arranged. After 50 years, the Giner family are still continually striving to improve the site and have added a spa and wellbeing facility and numerous activities, including pottery, silk painting, mosaics and water colours, and a beach club. A special area features Captain Farret's pirate ship, a range of children's activities and a special play area.

You might like to know

There's a wide variety of children's entertainment on offer here – dance classes, archery, fitness courses and much more.

- ✓ Multi-lingual children's club – pre-school
- ✓ Multi-lingual children's club – 5-10 year olds
- ✓ Multi-lingual children's club – 10-14 year olds
- ✓ Creative crafts
- ○ Bicycle hire for children
- ✓ Facilities for children in the wash blocks
- ✓ Children's pool
- ✓ Children's play area
- ○ Crèche and/or babysitting
- ✓ Local information of interest for children

Facilities: Very clean toilet blocks (one heated) have children's facilities and showers shaped like clowns! Baby rooms, facilities for disabled visitors. Washing machines. Dog shower. Motorcaravan services. Well stocked supermarket. Hairdresser. Bars with pizzas, snacks, takeaway. Restaurant. Crêperie with minigolf. Heated swimming pool complex (1,000 sq.m) with lifeguard all season. Wellness centre with sauna, steam room, jacuzzi etc. Gym. Excellent play areas. Miniclub (5-12 yrs). Teenagers' club (13-17 yrs). Tennis. Archery. Programme of games. Multisports court. Bicycle hire. WiFi (charged). Off site: Shops, bars and Luna Park within walking distance. Riding 1 km. Boat launching 6 km. Golf 10 km. Sailing and windsurfing on beach. Canal du Midi.

Open: 9 April - 26 September.

Directions: Site is south of Vias at Vias-Plage. From N112 (Béziers-Agde) take D137 signed Vias-Plage. Site is signed on the left.

GPS: 43.1727, 3.2507

Charges guide

Per unit incl. 2 persons
and electricity € 18,00 - € 57,00

extra person € 7,00 - € 9,00

dog € 5,00

Facilities:
Facilities: Good, modern toilet blocks include baby rooms, children's toilets, facilities for disabled visitors (whole site wheelchair friendly). En-suite facilities on payment. Washing machines and dryers. Motorcaravan services. Fridge hire. Large well stocked shop. Bar, restaurant and takeaway. Swimming pool complex (lifeguards all season). Good play area. Miniclub (4-8 yrs). Boules. New gym with sauna, games room, beauty salon and massage. Multisports court. Bicycle hire. Games/TV room. Variety of evening entertainment. WiFi throughout (charged). Communal barbecue (only gas and electric permitted on pitches). Off site: Fishing and riding 1 km. Portiragnes-Plage with beach bars and restaurants 2 km. Golf 10 km.

Open: 31 May - 6 September.

Directions: From A9 exit 35 (Béziers Est) take N112 south towards Sérignan (1 km). Large roundabout follow signs for Cap d'Agde, watch carefully for D37, Portiragnes (1-2 km), follow signs for Portiragnes-Plage. Site well signed before Portiragnes-Plage (5 km).

GPS: 43.29153, 3.37348

Charges guide

Per unit incl. 2 persons
and electricity € 21,00 - € 44,00

extra person € 5,00 - € 10,00

child (under 4 yrs) no charge - € 5,00

dog € 2,00 - € 6,00

private sanitary unit € 8,50 - € 11,00

Special offers for May and June.

Camping Caravaning les Mimosas

Port Cassafières, F-34420 Portiragnes-Plage (Hérault)
t: 04 67 90 92 92   e: les.mimosas.portiragnes@wanadoo.fr
alanrogers.com/FR34170   www.mimosas.com

Accommodation: ☑ Pitch   ☑ Mobile home/chalet   ○ Hotel/B&B   ○ Apartment

Les Mimosas is quite a large site with 400 pitches – 200 for touring units, the remainder for mobile homes – in a rural situation. The level, grassy pitches are of average size, separated and numbered in regular avenues, all with 6A electricity (long leads may be required), some have good shade, others have less. The pool area, a real feature of the site, includes a most impressive wave pool, various toboggans, the 'Space Hole' water slide, a large swimming pool and a super paddling pool (nine pools in all) with lots of free sun beds. This is a friendly, family run site with families in mind, with something new for each year. Les Mimosas has a less hectic situation than sites closer to the beach. However, it is possible to walk to a lovely sandy beach (1.2 km). There is lots going on and many day trips and excursions are arranged all season, from canoeing to visiting castles. Portiragnes-Plage is about 2 km. away and can be reached by cycle tracks. The Canal du Midi runs along the edge of the site (no access), providing another easy cycle route.

You might like to know

Dedicated staff will keep children (4-10 yrs) occupied with a range of activities throughout July and August. Bicycle hire, table tennis, paddling pool and slides, plus organised tournaments are just some of the activities on offer.

- ○ Multi-lingual children's club – pre-school
- ○ Multi-lingual children's club – 5-10 year olds
- ○ Multi-lingual children's club – 10-14 year olds
- ☑ Creative crafts
- ☑ Bicycle hire for children
- ☑ Facilities for children in the wash blocks
- ☑ Children's pool
- ☑ Children's play area
- ○ Crèche and/or babysitting
- ☑ Local information of interest for children

Camping les Sablons

Avenue des Muriers, F-34420 Portiragnes-Plage (Hérault)
t: 04 67 90 90 55   e: contact@les-sablons.com
alanrogers.com/FR34400   www.les-sablons.com

Accommodation: ☑ Pitch   ☑ Mobile home/chalet   ○ Hotel/B&B   ○ Apartment

Facilities: Well equipped, modernised toilet blocks include large showers, some with washbasins. Baby baths and facilities for disabled visitors. Supermarket, bakery and newsagent. Restaurant, bar and takeaway. Swimming pool complex. Entertainment and activity programme with sports, music and cultural activities. Children's club. Beach club. Tennis. Archery. Play areas. Bicycle hire. Electronic games. ATM. Internet access. WiFi throughout (charged). Off site: Village and bicycle hire 100 m. Beach and riding 200 m. Canal du Midi 1 km. Parc Adventure (high wire adventure park) 1.5 km.

Open: April - September.

Directions: From A9 exit 35 (Béziers Est) follow signs for Vias and Agde (N112). After large roundabout pass exit to Cers then take exit for Portiragnes (D37). Follow for 5 km. and pass over Canal du Midi towards Portiragnes-Plage. Site is on left after roundabout.

GPS: 43.28003, 3.36396

Charges guide

Per unit incl. 2 persons and electricity	€ 20,00 - € 52,00
extra person	€ 6,00 - € 10,00
child (under 13 yrs, acc. to age)	no charge - € 10,00
dog	€ 4,00

Les Sablons is an impressive and popular site with 680 pitches and lots going on, a village in itself. Most of the facilities are arranged around the entrance with shops, a restaurant, a bar and a large pool complex with no less than five slides and three heated pools. There is also direct access to a white sandy beach at the back of the site, close to a small lake. There is good shade on the majority of the site, although some of the newer touring pitches have less shade but are nearer the gate to the beach. On level sandy grass, all 220 touring pitches have 6A electricity. The remainder are taken by a range of mobile homes and chalets (many for hire, and a few for use by tour operators). A new entertainment office enables you to book a wide range of sporting, cultural and musical activities as well as excursions. Children's clubs, daily activities and evening entertainment are organised. In fact, this is a real holiday venue aiming to keep all the family happy. Some visitors simply stay on the site for their entire holiday – it certainly has everything.

You might like to know

Children will be spoiled for choice with 3 great playgrounds: the enormous Great Pyramid, the thrilling Tyrolean and the challenging Fort Sablons. After that, they can look forward to the water activities and miniclub (5-10 years).

- ○ Multi-lingual children's club – pre-school
- ☑ Multi-lingual children's club – 5-10 year olds
- ☑ Multi-lingual children's club – 10-14 year olds
- ☑ Creative crafts
- ○ Bicycle hire for children
- ☑ Facilities for children in the wash blocks
- ☑ Children's pool
- ☑ Children's play area
- ○ Crèche and/or babysitting
- ○ Local information of interest for children

Facilities:
Two modern toilet blocks provide unisex toilets, showers and washbasins in cubicles. Baby room. Facilities for disabled visitors recently improved. Laundry facilities. Shop, bar, restaurant and takeaway (all season). Motorcaravan services. Outdoor swimming pool with slide and new terrace surround (no Bermuda-style shorts; 1/5-15/9). Heated, covered pool (all season). Fitness room. Small play area. Games area. Boules. TV room. Bicycle hire (all season). Internet access. WiFi throughout (charged). Footpath to village. Off site: Tennis 200 m. Riding 5 km. Fishing 9 km. Golf 12 km.

Open: 3 April - 11 October.

Directions: Sonzay is northwest of Tours. From the new A28 north of Tours take exit 27 to Neuillé-Pont-Pierre which is on the D938 Le Mans-Tours road. Then take D766 towards Château la Vallière and turn southwest to Sonzay. Follow campsite signs.

GPS: 47.526228, 0.450865

Charges guide

Per unit incl. 2 persons
and electricity (10A) € 22,50 - € 32,00

extra person € 4,20 - € 5,80

child (3-12 yrs acc. to age)
no charge - € 4,00

dog € 2,50

Camping l'Arada Parc

Rue de la Baratière, F-37360 Sonzay (Indre-et-Loire)
t: 02 47 24 72 69 e: info@laradaparc.com
alanrogers.com/FR37060 www.laradaparc.com

Accommodation: ☑ Pitch ☑ Mobile home/chalet ○ Hotel/B&B ○ Apartment

A good, well maintained site in a quiet location, easy to find from the motorway and popular as an overnight stop, Camping l'Arada Parc is an attractive family site nestling in the heart of the Tourangelle countryside between the Loire and Loir valleys. The 62 grass touring pitches all have 10A electricity (Europlug) and 18 have water and drainage. The clearly marked pitches, some slightly sloping, are separated by trees and shrubs, some of which are handstanding and now provide a degree of shade. An attractive, heated pool is on a pleasant terrace beside the restaurant. Entertainment, themed evenings and activities for children are organised in July/August. This is a new site with modern facilities which include a superb covered pool and fitness room. The campsite is situated in the heart of 'château country' so you will have the opportunity to visit Villandry, Azay le Rideau and Langeais. Why not try the vineyards too? Chinon, Vouvray, Touraine and Amboise are nearby with plenty of tasting opportunities.

You might like to know

The indoor pool is open daily from 10am to 7pm, and the water is heated to 28°C. Activities on offer include aqua bike, elliptical bike, treadmill, and water aerobics in summer.

- ☑ Multi-lingual children's club – pre-school
- ☑ Multi-lingual children's club – 5-10 year olds
- ☑ Multi-lingual children's club – 10-14 year olds
- ☑ Creative crafts
- ○ Bicycle hire for children
- ☑ Facilities for children in the wash blocks
- ☑ Children's pool
- ☑ Children's play area
- ○ Crèche and/or babysitting
- ☑ Local information of interest for children

France – Les Abrets

Kawan Village le Coin Tranquille

6 chemin des Vignes, F-38490 Les Abrets (Isère)
t: 04 76 32 13 48 e: contact@coin-tranquille.com
alanrogers.com/FR38010 www.coin-tranquille.com

Accommodation: ☑ Pitch ☑ Mobile home/chalet ○ Hotel/B&B ○ Apartment

Le Coin Tranquille is well placed for visits to the Savoie regions and the Alps. It is an attractive, well maintained site of 192 grass pitches (178 for touring units), all with 10A electricity. They are separated by neat hedges of hydrangea, flowering shrubs and a range of trees to make a lovely environment doubly enhanced by the rural aspect and marvellous views across to the mountains. This is a popular, family run site with friendly staff, making it a wonderful base for exploring the area. Set in the Dauphiny countryside north of Grenoble, le Coin Tranquille is truly a quiet corner, especially outside school holiday times, although it is still popular with families in high season. The Chartreuse caves near Voiron are well worth a visit, as is the Monastery, and a mountain railway goes to the summit of the Chartreuse Massif. A comprehensive guide in English is given to guests on arrival detailing all the local scenic routes and places of interest.

You might like to know

There is an excellent children's club with a varied and imaginative activity programme throughout high season.

○ Multi-lingual children's club – pre-school
☑ Multi-lingual children's club – 5-10 year olds
☑ Multi-lingual children's club – 10-14 year olds
☑ Creative crafts
○ Bicycle hire for children
☑ Facilities for children in the wash blocks
☑ Children's pool
☑ Children's play area
○ Crèche and/or babysitting
☑ Local information of interest for children

Facilities: The central well appointed sanitary block is well kept, heated in low season. Facilities for disabled visitors. Two smaller blocks provide facilities in high season. Busy shop. Excellent restaurant. Heated swimming pool and paddling pool (1/5-30/9; no Bermuda-style shorts) with sunbathing areas. Play area. TV and games in bar. Quiet reading room. Weekly entertainment for children and adults (July/Aug) including live music (not discos). Bicycle hire (limited). WiFi near reception (free). Off site: Les Abrets with shops and supermarket 2 km. Riding 6 km. Fishing 8 km. Golf 30 km.

Open: 1 April - 1 November.

Directions: Les Abrets is 70 km. southeast of Lyon at junction of D1006 (previously N6) and D1075 (previously N75). From roundabout in town take N6 towards Chambéry, turning left in just under 2 km. (signed restaurant and camping). Follow signs along country lane for just over 1 km. and entrance is on right.

GPS: 45.54115, 5.60778

Charges guide

Per unit incl. 2 persons and electricity	€ 21,00 - € 37,50
extra person	€ 4,00 - € 8,00
child (2-7 yrs)	€ 2,50 - € 5,00
dog	€ 2,00

Facilities: Four main toilet blocks and two smaller blocks are comfortable and clean with facilities for babies and disabled visitors. Motorcaravan services. Fridge rental. Well stocked shop and bar (all season). Restaurant, takeaway (1/6-7/9). Stage for live shows arranged in July/Aug. Outdoor swimming pool, paddling pool (all season) and heated, covered pool (May-July). Tennis. Multisports court. Bicycle hire. WiFi (charged). Charcoal barbecues are not permitted. Off site: Riding (July/Aug) 500 m. Surf school 500 m. Beach and fishing 700 m. Golf 18 km.

Open: 12 May - 13 September.

Directions: Turn off D652 at St Girons on D42 towards St Girons-Plage. Site is on left before coming to beach (4.5 km).

GPS: 43.95166, -1.35212

Charges guide

Per unit incl. 2 persons
and electricity € 20,00 - € 39,00

extra person (over 5 yrs) € 6,00

dog € 4,00

France – Saint Girons-Plage

Camping Club International Eurosol

Route de la Plage, F-40560 Saint Girons-Plage (Landes)
t: 05 58 47 90 14 e: contact@camping-eurosol.com
alanrogers.com/FR40060 www.camping-eurosol.com

Accommodation: ☑ Pitch ☑ Mobile home/chalet ○ Hotel/B&B ○ Apartment

Privately owned, Eurosol is an attractive, friendly and well maintained site extending over 15 hectares of undulating ground amongst mature pine trees giving good shade. Of the 356 touring pitches, 231 have electricity (10A) with 120 fully serviced. A wide range of mobile homes and chalets, which are being updated, are available for rent. This is very much a family site with multi-lingual entertainers. Many games and tournaments are organised and a beach volleyball competition is held regularly in front of the bar. The adjacent boules terrain is floodlit. An excellent sandy beach 700 metres from the site has supervised bathing in high season and is ideal for surfing. The landscaped swimming pool complex is impressive with three large pools, one of which is covered and heated, and a large children's paddling pool. There is a convivial restaurant and takeaway food service. A large supermarket is well stocked with fresh bread daily and international newspapers.

You might like to know

This safe, peaceful family campsite in the shade of a pine forest is the ideal holiday destination for the whole family. With plenty to keep the youngsters busy, parents can enjoy a relaxing break.

○ Multi-lingual children's club – pre-school

☑ Multi-lingual children's club – 5-10 year olds

☑ Multi-lingual children's club – 10-14 year olds

☑ Creative crafts

☑ Bicycle hire for children

☑ Facilities for children in the wash blocks

☑ Children's pool

☑ Children's play area

○ Crèche and/or babysitting

☑ Local information of interest for children

Facilities: Three modern sanitary blocks include some washbasins in cabins and baby bathrooms. Laundry facilities. Facilities for disabled visitors. Motorcaravan services. Shop. Restaurant. Takeaway in bar with terrace. Pool complex. Spa centre. 7-hectare lake (fishing, bathing, canoes, pedalos, cable-ski). 9-hole golf course. Adventure play area. Tennis. Minigolf. Boules. Roller skating/skateboarding (bring own equipment). Bicycle hire. Internet access and WiFi (charged). Off site: Riding 6 km.

Open: 2 May - 6 September.

Directions: From A71, take Lamotte-Beuvron exit (no 3) or from N20 Orléans to Vierzon turn left on to D923 towards Aubigny. After 14 km. turn right at camping sign on to D24E. Site signed in 2 km.

GPS: 47.54398, 2.19193

Charges guide

Per unit incl. 2 persons
and electricity € 20,00 - € 46,00

extra person € 7,00 - € 10,00

child (1-17 yrs acc. to age)
no charge - € 9,00

dog € 5,00 - € 7,00

Reductions for low season longer stays.

France – Pierrefitte-sur-Sauldre

Leading Camping les Alicourts

Domaine des Alicourts, F-41300 Pierrefitte-sur-Sauldre (Loir-et-Cher)
t: 02 54 88 63 34 e: info@lesalicourts.com
alanrogers.com/FR41030 www.lesalicourts.com

Accommodation: ☑ Pitch ☑ Mobile home/chalet ○ Hotel/B&B ○ Apartment

A secluded holiday village set in the heart of the forest, with many sporting facilities and a super spa centre, Camping les Alicourts is midway between Orléans and Bourges, to the east of the A71. There are 490 pitches, 153 for touring and the remainder occupied by mobile homes and chalets. All pitches have 6A electricity connections and good provision for water, and most are 150 sq.m. (min. 100 sq.m). Locations vary, from wooded to more open areas, thus giving a choice of amount of shade. All facilities are open all season and the leisure amenities are exceptional. The Senseo Balnéo centre offers indoor pools, hydrotherapy, massage and spa treatments for over 18s only (some special family sessions are provided). An inviting, part-covered outdoor water complex (all season) includes two swimming pools, a pool with wave machine and a beach area, not forgetting three water slides. Competitions and activities are organised for adults and children, including a high season club for children with an entertainer twice a day, a disco once a week and a dance for adults. A member of Leading Campings group.

You might like to know

There is a mini disco for children every evening, and during high season they are kept entertained by shows, including one they can star in themselves!

○ Multi-lingual children's club – pre-school
☑ Multi-lingual children's club – 5-10 year olds
☑ Multi-lingual children's club – 10-14 year olds
○ Creative crafts
☑ Bicycle hire for children
☑ Facilities for children in the wash blocks
☑ Children's pool
☑ Children's play area
○ Crèche and/or babysitting
○ Local information of interest for children

Camping le Fief

57 chemin du Fief, F-44250 Saint Brévin-les-Pins (Loire-Atlantique)
t: 02 40 27 23 86 e: camping@lefief.com
alanrogers.com/FR44190 www.lefief.com

Accommodation: ☑ Pitch ☑ Mobile home/chalet ○ Hotel/B&B ○ Apartment

If you are a family with young children or lively teenagers, this could be the campsite for you. Le Fief is a well established site only 800 m. from sandy beaches on the southern Brittany coast. It has a magnificent aquapark with outdoor and covered swimming pools, paddling pools, slides, river rapids, fountains, jets and more. The site has 125 pitches for touring units, all with 8A electricity and varying slightly in size and accessibility. There are also 205 mobile homes and chalets to rent and 40 privately owned units. An impressive Taos mobile home village includes a new Sunny Club for children. There is a variety of entertainment and organised activity for all ages which ranges from a miniclub for 4-12 year olds, to Tonic Days in a state-of-the-art wellness centre with aquagym, jogging and sports competitions, and to evening events which include karaoke, themed dinners and cabaret. There are plenty of sporting facilities for active youngsters. There are numerous sandy beaches along the Jade Coast, and across the bay to the south is the island of Noirmoutier.

You might like to know

Miniclub and Club Junior (4-12 yrs) are available during weekends and holidays from April to September.

- ○ Multi-lingual children's club – pre-school
- ☑ Multi-lingual children's club – 5-10 year olds
- ☑ Multi-lingual children's club – 10-14 year olds
- ○ Creative crafts
- ☑ Bicycle hire for children
- ☑ Facilities for children in the wash blocks
- ☑ Children's pool
- ☑ Children's play area
- ○ Crèche and/or babysitting
- ☑ Local information of interest for children

Facilities: One excellent new toilet block and three others of a lower standard. Laundry facilities. Shop (30/6-31/8). Bar, restaurant and takeaway (12/4-28/9) with terrace overlooking the pool complex. Heated outdoor pools, etc. (1/5-15/9). Covered pool (all season). Wellness centre. Play area. Tennis. Pétanque. Archery. Games room. Organised entertainment and activities (weekends April/June, daily July/Aug). Bicycle hire. WiFi over site (charged). Off site: Shops, bars and restaurants nearby. Beach 800 m. Bus stop 1 km. Fishing 2 km. Boat launching and riding 1 km. Golf 15 km. Planète Sauvage safari park.

Open: 12 April - 28 September.

Directions: From the St Nazaire bridge take the fourth exit from the D213 signed St Brévin-l'Océan. Continue over first roundabout and bear right at the second to join Chemin du Fief. The site is on the right, well signed.

GPS: 47.23486, -2.16757

Charges guide

Per unit incl. 2 persons and electricity	€ 25,00 - € 47,00
extra person	€ 6,00 - € 11,00
child (0-7 yrs)	€ 3,00 - € 5,50
dog	€ 5,00 - € 10,00

No credit cards.

Facilities: The two sanitary blocks are clean and well maintained. Facilities for disabled visitors. Washing machine. Motorcaravan services. Excellent gift shop selling regional and local produce (bread available). Bar, restaurant and takeaway. Swimming pool and paddling pool. TV and games rooms. Boules. Bicycle hire. Play area. Small library. Weekly soirées in high season. Charcoal barbecues are not permitted. Free WiFi over part of site. Max. 2 small dogs. Off site: Fishing 3 km. Golf 8 km. Riding 15 km.

Open: 5 April - 28 September.

Directions: From the A20 take exit 56 and follow D2 towards St Germain-du-Bel-Air. Continue for 5 km. and the site is on the right.

GPS: 44.69197, 1.53461

Charges guide

Per unit incl. 2 persons and electricity	€ 19,50 - € 30,00
extra person	€ 4,50 - € 7,00
child (1-7 yrs)	€ 3,50 - € 5,00
dog	€ 2,50 - € 3,00

France – Séniergues

Domaine de la Faurie

F-46240 Séniergues (Lot)
t: 05 65 21 14 36   e: contact@camping-lafaurie.com
alanrogers.com/FR46190   www.camping-lafaurie.com

Accommodation: ☑ Pitch   ☑ Mobile home/chalet   ○ Hotel/B&B   ○ Apartment

A stunning array of tended shrubs and thoughtful flower planting is spread throughout this very pretty seven-hectare site, which is located on a hilltop with wide open views of the surrounding hills and valleys. Although hidden away, it is an excellent base for exploring the Lot and Dordogne regions. The site is separated into two distinct areas, an open, lightly shaded front section and a much more densely shaded area with tall pine trees all around the pitches. The 54 touring pitches, with 6A electricity, are large and most are at least 100 sq.m. A small number also have water and drainage. The friendly French owners will tell you that they consider the site their personal garden. This accounts for the beautiful presentation. The section of mobile homes, each with its own planted garden, blends in very well with the surroundings. The wooded section of pitches particularly (total 54 touring), has small paths and tight turns which could cause difficulties for larger units.

You might like to know

Every morning, the children are kept busy with games and craft workshops. The older ones will enjoy zumba classes on Wednesday afternoons.

- ○ Multi-lingual children's club – pre-school
- ☑ Multi-lingual children's club – 5-10 year olds
- ○ Multi-lingual children's club – 10-14 year olds
- ☑ Creative crafts
- ○ Bicycle hire for children
- ☑ Facilities for children in the wash blocks
- ☑ Children's pool
- ☑ Children's play area
- ○ Crèche and/or babysitting
- ○ Local information of interest for children

Facilities: Three modern toilet blocks with all necessary facilities including those for babies and disabled campers. Washing up sinks and laundry. Shop and épicerie. Restaurant, pizzeria and takeaway (all season). Outdoor swimming pool (22/5-27/8) and heated indoor swimming pool (2/5-15/9). Tennis. Multisports pitch. Go-karts. Minigolf. Bicycle hire. Games and TV rooms. Varied sporting and entertainment programme (10/7-25/8). Pony riding. Torch useful. WiFi over site (charged; free in reception area). Off site: Boat launching 5 km. Golf 7 km.

Open: 19 April - 15 September.

Directions: Site is well signed on the north bank of the River Loire, 100 m. north of the main D952, Saumur-Tours road, 5 km. northeast of Saumur.

GPS: 47.24731, -0.00048

Charges guide

Per unit incl. 2 persons
and electricity € 17,50 - € 38,00

with water and drainage € 19,00 - € 40,50

extra person € 6,50 - € 8,50

child (4-12 yrs) € 4,00 - € 4,50

Castel Camping Domaine de la Brèche

5 impasse de la Brèche (RN152), F-49730 Varennes-sur-Loire (Maine-et-Loire)
t: 02 41 51 22 92 e: contact@domainedelabreche.com
alanrogers.com/FR49010 www.domainedelabreche.com

Accommodation: ☑ Pitch ☑ Mobile home/chalet ○ Hotel/B&B ○ Apartment

The Saint Cast family have developed Domaine de la Brèche with care and attention. The attractive site occupies a 24-hectare estate, 4 km. northeast of Saumur on the edge of the Loire behind the dykes. There are 235 spacious, level, grass pitches, with 135 for touring. Trees and bushes give some shade. All have electricity (some require long cables). Eighty have a water supply and drainage. The restaurant, bar and terrace, also open to the public, provide a social base and are popular with British visitors. The pool complex includes one with a removable cover, one outdoor, and one for toddlers. It is a good base from which to explore the famous châteaux, abbeys, wine cellars, mushroom caves and Troglodyte villages in this region. The site includes a small lake (used for fishing) and wooded area ensuring a quiet, relaxed and rural atmosphere and making Domaine de la Brèche a comfortable holiday base for couples and families.

You might like to know

Pony rides and lessons with an instructor are available.

- ☑ Multi-lingual children's club – pre-school
- ☑ Multi-lingual children's club – 5-10 year olds
- ○ Multi-lingual children's club – 10-14 year olds
- ☑ Creative crafts
- ○ Bicycle hire for children
- ☑ Facilities for children in the wash blocks
- ☑ Children's pool
- ☑ Children's play area
- ○ Crèche and/or babysitting
- ☑ Local information of interest for children

Facilities: Nine modern sanitary blocks are very well equipped and maintained, with British style WCs and washbasins in cabins. Good facilities for children and for disabled campers. Laundry room. Motorcaravan services. Range of shops. Gas supplies. Bars and restaurant. New pool complex (heated). Play areas. Sports field. Tennis. Sporting activities. Library, games and video room. Hairdresser. Internet café and WiFi. Daily entertainment programme. Bicycle hire. Fishing. ATM. Exchange facilities. Post office. Weather forecasts. Free WiFi in bar. Only gas or electric barbecues are allowed. Off site: Boat launching and sailing 500 m. Riding 5 km. Golf 12 km.

Open: 11 April - 3 October.

Directions: From A9 exit 41 (Perpignan Centre, Rivesaltes) follow signs for Le Barcarès and Canet on D83 for 10 km. then for Canet (D81). At first Canet roundabout, turn fully back on yourself (Ste Marie) and watch for Brasilia sign almost immediately on right.

GPS: 42.70467, 3.03483

Charges guide

Per unit incl. 2 persons and electricity (6A)	€ 24,00 - € 61,00
extra person	€ 6,50 - € 9,00
child (3-6 yrs)	no charge
dog (max. 2)	€ 5,00

No credit cards.

France – Canet-en-Roussillon

Yelloh! Village le Brasilia

2 avenue Anneaux du Roussillon, F-66141 Canet-en-Roussillon (Pyrénées-Orientales)
t: 04 68 80 23 82   e: info@lebrasilia.fr
alanrogers.com/FR66070   www.brasilia.fr

Accommodation: ✔ Pitch   ✔ Mobile home/chalet   ○ Hotel/B&B   ○ Apartment

Situated across the yacht harbour from the resort of Canet-Plage, le Brasilia is an impressive, well managed family site directly beside the beach. Although large, it is pretty, neat and well kept with an amazingly wide range of facilities – indeed, it is camping at its best. There are 421 neatly hedged touring pitches, all with electricity (6-10A) and 304 with water and drainage. They vary in size from 80 to 120 sq.m. and some of the longer pitches are suitable for two families together. There is a variety of shade from pines and flowering shrubs, with less on pitches near the beach. There are 288 pitches with mobile homes and chalets to rent (the new ones have their own gardens). The sandy beach here is busy, with a beach club and a naturist section to the west of the site. An exciting pool complex with pools catering for all ages and hydrotherapy facilities for adults is overlooked by its own snack bar and restaurant. A new state-of-the-art reception and information centre was completed in 2012. A member of Yelloh! Village and Leading Campings group.

You might like to know

Spain is very close and day trips to towns such as Figueras (Dali Museum), Girona or even Barcelona are possible.

✔ Multi-lingual children's club – pre-school

✔ Multi-lingual children's club – 5-10 year olds

✔ Multi-lingual children's club – 10-14 year olds

✔ Creative crafts

✔ Bicycle hire for children

✔ Facilities for children in the wash blocks

✔ Children's pool

✔ Children's play area

○ Crèche and/or babysitting

✔ Local information of interest for children

Facilities: Four fully equipped toilet blocks on le Floride and two on l'Embouchure where 50 pitches near the beach have individual facilities. Facilities for babies and disabled visitors. Family shower room. Motorcaravan services. Shop, bar, restaurant and takeaway (all 15/6-5/9). Excellent pool complex with indoor heated pool. Excellent play area. Multisports court. Gym. Tennis. Multi-lingual entertainment and sports programmes (1/5-30/9). Bicycle hire. Charcoal barbecues are not permitted. Max. 1 dog. WiFi over site (charged). Off site: Beach 100 m. Fishing 1 km. Riding 1.5 km.

Open: 1 April - 30 September.

Directions: From A9 take exit 41 (Perpignan Nord) and follow signs for Canet and Le Barcarès via D83. At exit 9 follow D81 (Canet) then next left into Le Barcarès Village. Site is 1 km. on the left and right sides of the road.

GPS: 42.77855, 3.0301

Charges guide

Per unit incl. 2 persons and electricity	€ 15,00 - € 43,70
incl. individual sanitary facility	€ 19,00 - € 54,30
extra person	€ 2,90 - € 6,70
child (1-3 yrs)	no charge - € 3,90

France – Le Barcarès

Camping Club le Floride et l'Embouchure

Route de Saint Laurent, F-66423 Le Barcarès (Pyrénées-Orientales)
t: 04 68 86 11 75 e: campingfloride@orange.fr
alanrogers.com/FR66290 www.floride.fr

Accommodation: ☑ Pitch ☑ Mobile home/chalet ○ Hotel/B&B ○ Apartment

A well established and multi-lingual, family run enterprise, le Floride et l'Embouchure is really two sites in one – l'Embouchure the smaller one with direct access to the beach and le Floride on the opposite side of the road. Fifty pitches have their own individual sanitary facility and in total the site offers 632 reasonably sized pitches, 280 for touring, all with 10A electricity. A good range of chalets and mobile homes are available for rent, including a recent Polynesian-style village. It is relatively inexpensive, especially outside the July/August peak period and the majority of the comprehensive facilities are open from May. The busy town of Le Barcarès is within easy walking distance and has an increasing range of shops and supermarkets. The Voie Verte tarmac pathway runs for 15 km. from Le Barcarès to Rivesaltes alongside the River Agly, which borders l'Embouchure and is popular with cyclists, walkers, runners and roller skaters.

You might like to know

The site has direct access to the sea (100 m) and to a 3,000 sq.m. aquatic complex with covered, heated swimming pool, paddling pool with games, a jacuzzi and fun slides.

☑ Multi-lingual children's club – pre-school
☑ Multi-lingual children's club – 5-10 year olds
☑ Multi-lingual children's club – 10-14 year olds
☑ Creative crafts
☑ Bicycle hire for children
☑ Facilities for children in the wash blocks
☑ Children's pool
☑ Children's play area
○ Crèche and/or babysitting
☑ Local information of interest for children

Facilities: Excellent refurbished, heated toilet blocks. Individual toilet units on 18 pitches. Facilities for disabled visitors. Laundry room. Motorcaravan services. Shop. Gift shop. Takeaway. Bar/restaurant. Five circular swimming pools (two heated), one for adults, one for children (covered and heated), three arranged as a waterfall (all season). Spa with sauna, etc. Disco. Archery. Minigolf. Tennis. Pony rides. Pétanque. Squash. Playground. Nursery. Bicycle hire. Internet access. Events are organised in season. No barbecues. WiFi throughout. Baby club (3 months to 3 years) all season. Off site: Golf nearby. Trekking by foot, bicycle or pony in l'Esterel forest park. Fishing and beach 3 km.

Open: 5 April - 27 September.

Directions: From A8, exit Fréjus, follow signs for Valescure, then for Agay, site is on left. The road from Agay is the easiest to follow but it is possible to approach from St Raphaël via Valescure. Look carefully for site sign, which is difficult to see.

GPS: 43.453775, 6.832817

Charges guide

Per unit incl. 2 persons and electricity	€ 18,00 - € 38,00
extra person	€ 9,00 - € 11,00
child (acc. to age)	€ 5,00 - € 10,00
dog	€ 4,00

France – Agay

Camping Caravaning Esterel

Avenue des Golfs, Agay, F-83530 Saint Raphaël (Var)
t: 04 94 82 03 28 e: contact@esterel-caravaning.fr
alanrogers.com/FR83020 www.esterel-caravaning.co.uk

Accommodation: ⊘ Pitch ⊘ Mobile home/chalet ○ Hotel/B&B ○ Apartment

Esterel is a quality, award-winning caravan site east of Saint Raphaël, set among the hills beyond Agay. The site is 3.5 km. from the sandy beach at Agay where parking is perhaps a little easier than at most places on this coast, but a shuttle runs from the site to and from the beach several times daily in July and August (€ 1). It has 164 touring pitches for caravans but not tents; all have 10A electricity and a water tap, 18 special ones have their own en-suite washroom adjoining whilst others also have a washing machine, a dishwasher, a jacuzzi, 16A electricity and free WiFi. Pitches are on shallow terraces, attractively landscaped with good shade and a variety of flowers, giving a feeling of spaciousness. Developed by the Laroche family for over 30 years, the site has an attractive, quiet situation with good views of the Esterel mountains. This is a very good site, well run and organised in a popular area. Great efforts have been made over the last year to improve the site's 'green credentials', including the planting of over 5,000 flowering shrubs in 2012.

You might like to know

Clubs for babies, children and teenagers (3 months - 17 years) are free in April, May and September and provide non-stop entertainment and activities. Baby kits are available to hire (free in June).

- ⊘ Multi-lingual children's club – pre-school
- ⊘ Multi-lingual children's club – 5-10 year olds
- ⊘ Multi-lingual children's club – 10-14 year olds
- ⊘ Creative crafts
- ⊘ Bicycle hire for children
- ⊘ Facilities for children in the wash blocks
- ⊘ Children's pool
- ⊘ Children's play area
- ⊘ Crèche and/or babysitting
- ⊘ Local information of interest for children

Facilities: Five toilet blocks. Supermarket, several shops. Two bars, terrace overlooking pools, TV. Restaurant, takeaway, pizzeria. Six swimming pools (heated all season), one aquatic playground for children up to four years, two covered, plus steam room and jacuzzi, seven slides. Fitness centre. Tennis. Archery (July/Aug). Skateboard park. Organised events, daytime and evening entertainment, some in English. Amphitheatre. Discos all season. Children's club (all season, 4-11 yrs). Two renovated play areas. WiFi (charged). Off site: Bus to Fréjus passes gate. Riding 2 km. Golf and beach 5 km. Fishing 8 km.

Open: 28 March - 26 September.

Directions: From west on A8, exit 38 'Fréjus centre' and right at first roundabout onto D4a, right at second roundabout, right at the crossroads onto D4 and site is 1 km. on the left.

GPS: 43.45998, 6.72048

Charges guide

Per unit incl. 2 persons, electricity, water and drainage € 19,00 - € 51,00

extra person € 5,00 - € 14,00

child (under 7 yrs) no charge - € 8,00

dog € 5,00

Min. stay for motorcaravans 2 nights. Large units should book.

Camping Resort la Baume-la Palmeraie

3775 rue des Combattants d'Afrique du Nord, F-83618 Fréjus (Var)
t: 04 94 19 88 88   e: reception@labaume-lapalmeraie.com
alanrogers.com/FR83060   www.labaume-lapalmeraie.com

Accommodation: ☑ Pitch   ☑ Mobile home/chalet   ○ Hotel/B&B   ☑ Apartment

La Baume is a large, busy site about 5.5 km. from the long sandy beach of Fréjus-Plage, although with its fine and varied selection of swimming pools many people do not bother to make the trip. The pools, with their palm trees, are remarkable for their size and variety (water slides, etc) – the very large feature pool being a highlight. There is also an aquatic play area and two indoor pools with a slide and a spa area. The site has 240 adequately sized, fully serviced pitches with some separators and most have shade. Although tents are accepted, the site concentrates mainly on caravanning. It becomes full in season. Adjoining la Baume is its sister site, la Palmeraie, providing self-catering accommodation, its own landscaped pool and some entertainment to supplement that at la Baume. There are 500 large pitches with mains sewerage for mobile homes. La Baume's convenient location has its downside – traffic noise on some pitches from the nearby autoroute.

You might like to know

There are two playgrounds on site, a mini disco every week and a miniclub for children aged 4 to 11 from April to September. There is trampolining and a circus in July and August, and evening entertainment for the whole family.

○ Multi-lingual children's club – pre-school

☑ Multi-lingual children's club – 5-10 year olds

☑ Multi-lingual children's club – 10-14 year olds

☑ Creative crafts

☑ Bicycle hire for children

☑ Facilities for children in the wash blocks

☑ Children's pool

☑ Children's play area

○ Crèche and/or babysitting

☑ Local information of interest for children

Facilities:

Facilities: Ten modern, well used but clean toilet blocks. Mostly Turkish WCs. Facilities for disabled visitors (but steep steps). Baby room. Washing machines. Fridge hire. Well stocked supermarket, bars, pizzeria (all open all season). No swimming pool. Several excellent play areas for all ages. Activities and entertainment for children and teenagers (July/Aug). Tennis. Boats, pedalos for hire. Wide range of watersports. New water games and fitness area. Multisports courts (one indoor for wet or hot weather) for football, basketball. Only gas and electric barbecues are allowed. Direct beach access. Dogs are not accepted 12/7-16/8. Free WiFi at the Tennis Bar (rest of site charged). Off site: Bicycle hire 2.5 km. Riding and golf 15 km.

Open: 28 March - 31 October.

Directions: From Bormes-les-Mimosas, head east on D559 to Le Lavandou. At roundabout, turn off D559 towards the sea on road signed Favière. After 2 km. turn left at site signs.

GPS: 43.11779, 6.35176

Charges guide

Per unit incl. 2 persons and electricity	€ 31,00 - € 49,00
extra person	€ 6,50 - € 11,50
child (2-7 yrs)	no charge - € 5,60
dog (not 13/7-17/8)	no charge

France – Bormes-les-Mimosas

Camp du Domaine

B.P. 207 La Favière, 2581 Route de Bénat, F-83230 Bormes-les-Mimosas (Var)
t: 04 94 71 03 12   e: mail@campdudomaine.com
alanrogers.com/FR83120   www.campdudomaine.com

Accommodation: ☑ Pitch ☑ Mobile home/chalet ○ Hotel/B&B ○ Apartment

Camp du Domaine, 3 km. south of Le Lavandou, is a large, attractive beachside site with 1,320 pitches set in 45 hectares of pinewood, yet surprisingly it does not give the impression of being so big. The pitches are large and most are reasonably level; 800 have 10A electricity. The most popular pitches are beside the beach, but those furthest away are generally larger and have more shade. Amongst the trees, many pitches are more suitable for tents. The price for each pitch is the same – whether smaller but near the beach, or larger under shade. The beach is the attraction and everyone tries to get close. American motorhomes are not accepted. Despite its size, the site does not feel too busy, except perhaps around the supermarket. This is mainly because many pitches are hidden in the trees, the access roads are quite wide and it all covers quite a wide area (some of the beach pitches are 600 m. from the entrance). Its popularity makes early reservation necessary over a long season (about mid June to mid September) since regular clients book from season to season. A member of Leading Campings group.

You might like to know

The free miniclub (7-14 years) runs creative activities and sports led by qualified youth leaders. In the evening, younger campers are entertained by puppet shows and circus-style performances.

- ○ Multi-lingual children's club – pre-school
- ☑ Multi-lingual children's club – 5-10 year olds
- ☑ Multi-lingual children's club – 10-14 year olds
- ☑ Creative crafts
- ○ Bicycle hire for children
- ☑ Facilities for children in the wash blocks
- ○ Children's pool
- ☑ Children's play area
- ○ Crèche and/or babysitting
- ☑ Local information of interest for children

Facilities: Four toilet blocks with very good facilities for campers with disabilities, some have hot showers in the open air. Superb children's section. Shop, bar, excellent restaurant/takeaway, swimming pools, hydrotherapy centre (all open 12/4-5/10). Sauna. Tennis. Adventure play area. Activities all season. Archery. Guided walks. Children's club. Only gas barbecues are allowed. WiFi throughout (charged). Pets are not accepted. Off site: Bédoin with shops and restaurants 1.5 km. Discover the riches of Provence with its many interesting old market towns and villages. Superb area for walking and cycling with the challenge of Mont Ventoux. Bicycle hire 2 km.

Open: 13 April - 10 October.

Directions: From A7 autoroute (exit 22) or RN7, south of Orange, take D950 southeast to Carpentras, then D974 northeast to Bédoin. In Bédoin turn right at roundabout, site is in 2 km. and signed.

GPS: 44.13352, 5.18745

Charges guide

Per unit incl. 2 persons
and electricity € 28,10 - € 46,60

extra person € 6,60 - € 10,00

child (3-8 yrs) no charge - € 9,80

Various offers and reductions
outside high season.

Domaine Naturiste de Bélézy

132 chemin de Maraval, F-84410 Bedoin (Vaucluse)
t: 04 90 65 60 18 e: info@belezy.com
alanrogers.com/FR84020 www.belezy.com

Accommodation: ✔ Pitch ✔ Mobile home/chalet ○ Hotel/B&B ○ Apartment

At the foot of Mont Ventoux, surrounded by beautiful scenery, Bélézy is an excellent naturist site with many amenities and activities and the ambience is relaxed and comfortable. The 326 pitches, 248 for touring (12A electricity, long leads required) are set amongst many varieties of trees and shrubs giving space and privacy. The attractive bar/restaurant and terrace overlook the swimming pool area and have superb views over the large recreational area and hills beyond. The site has an ecological theme with a small farm, a fish pond and a vegetable garden especially for the children. Near the pool area is a smart restaurant, with terrace, and the mellow old Mas (Provençal farmhouse) that houses many of the activities and amenities. There is a hydrotherapy centre to tone up and revitalise, with qualified diagnosis, including steam baths, massage and seaweed packs, osteopathy, Chinese medicine (including acupuncture) and Bach therapies. Activities are arranged including painting, pottery courses and language lessons and music (bring your own instrument).

You might like to know

An educational farm runs during summer with animals and an organic kitchen garden (with children's cookery lessons using home-grown produce). Special lodge tents can be rented for children from 6-13 years.

- ✔ Multi-lingual children's club – pre-school
- ✔ Multi-lingual children's club – 5-10 year olds
- ✔ Multi-lingual children's club – 10-14 year olds
- ✔ Creative crafts
- ✔ Bicycle hire for children
- ✔ Facilities for children in the wash blocks
- ✔ Children's pool
- ✔ Children's play area
- ✔ Crèche and/or babysitting
- ✔ Local information of interest for children

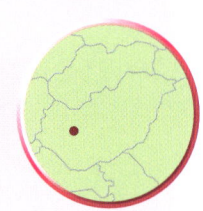

Facilities: The three excellent, well equipped sanitary blocks have child sized toilets and washbasins. Two bathrooms (hourly charge). Heated baby room. Facilities for disabled campers. Launderette. Dog shower. Motorcaravan services. Supermarket, souvenir shop and several bars (all 1/6-31/8). Restaurants. Children's pool (1/6-31/8). Massage. Hairdresser. Sports field. Minigolf. Fishing. Bicycle hire. Canoe, rowing boat and pedalo hire. Extensive entertainment programme for all ages. WiFi throughout (one free zone, elsewhere charged). Off site: Riding 3 km. Golf 20 km.

Open: 25 April - 28 September.

Directions: Follow road 71 from Veszprém southeast to Keszthely. Site is in Révfülöp.

GPS: 46.829469, 17.640164

Charges guide

Per unit incl. 2 persons and electricity	HUF 3750 - 7300
extra person	HUF 900 - 1250
child (2-14 yrs)	HUF 550 - 1000
dog	HUF 550 - 1000

Hungary – Révfülöp

Balatontourist Camping Napfény

Halász ut. 5, H-8253 Révfülöp (Veszprem County)
t: 87 563 031 e: napfeny@balatontourist.hu
alanrogers.com/HU5370 www.balatontourist.hu

Accommodation: ✓ Pitch ✓ Mobile home/chalet ○ Hotel/B&B ○ Apartment

Camping Napfény, an exceptionally good site, is designed for families with children of all ages looking for an active holiday, and has a 200 m. frontage on Lake Balaton. The site's 370 pitches vary in size (60-110 sq.m) and almost all have shade – very welcome during the hot Hungarian summers – and 6/10A electricity. As with most of the sites on Lake Balaton, a train line runs just outside the site boundary. There are steps to get into the lake and canoes, boats and pedalos for hire. An extensive entertainment programme is designed for all ages and there are several bars and restaurants of various styles. There are souvenir shops and a supermarket. In fact, you need not leave the site at all during your holiday, although there are several excursions on offer, including to Budapest or to one of the many Hungarian spas, a trip over Lake Balaton or a traditional wine tour.

You might like to know

Camping Napfény is in a great location with direct access to Lake Balaton, where children can safely play on the small, sandy beach.

- ✓ Multi-lingual children's club – pre-school
- ○ Multi-lingual children's club – 5-10 year olds
- ✓ Multi-lingual children's club – 10-14 year olds
- ✓ Creative crafts
- ✓ Bicycle hire for children
- ✓ Facilities for children in the wash blocks
- ✓ Children's pool
- ✓ Children's play area
- ○ Crèche and/or babysitting
- ✓ Local information of interest for children

Facilities: Two high quality, fully equipped sanitary blocks include private cabins, family shower rooms and facilities for disabled visitors. Washing machines. Shop. Restaurant with TV. Bar beside beach. Heated swimming pool with flumes. Gym. Small playground, miniclub and children's disco. Bicycle hire. WiFi (charged). Only gas and electric barbecues permitted on individual pitches; charcoal only permitted in the designated area. Dogs are not accepted. Off site: Use of facilities at IT60200 Union Lido (extra charge for pool). Sports centre, golf and riding 400 m. Venice.

Open: 23 April - 20 September.

Directions: From Venice-Trieste A4 autostrada leave at exit for airport or Quarto d'Altino and follow signs for Jesolo and Punta Sabbioni. Site well signed on left after Cavallino.

GPS: 45.46836, 12.53338

Charges guide

Per unit incl. 2 persons
and electricity € 21,80 - € 48,70

extra person € 4,80 - € 9,60

child (1-5 yrs) no charge - € 6,90

Three charging seasons.

Italy – *Cavallino-Treporti*

Italy Camping Village

Via Fausta 272, I-30013 Cavallino-Treporti (Veneto)
t: 041 968 090 e: info@campingitaly.it
alanrogers.com/IT60210 www.campingitaly.it

Accommodation: ☑ Pitch ☑ Mobile home/chalet ○ Hotel/B&B ○ Apartment

Italy Camping Village, under the same ownership as the better known Union Lido which it adjoins, is suggested for those who prefer a smaller, more compact site. The 180 touring pitches are on either side of sand tracks off hard access roads under a cover of trees. All have electricity connections (10A Europlug) and 126 are fully serviced. Pitches are between 50-100 sq.m. but access is impossible for large units, particularly in high season when cars are parked everywhere. A pleasant heated swimming pool (with lifeguard) has two slides, one is very long. There is direct access to a gently sloping sandy beach. A pleasant, heated, swimming pool has a slide and a whirlpool at one end, but for those who want a greater choice of activities, guests can use the facilities at Union Lido for a small additional charge. Strict regulations regarding undue noise here make this a relatively peaceful site and with lower charges than some in the area, this would be a good choice for families with young children. Advance booking is possible.

You might like to know

There is a great new children's playground on the beach.

○ Multi-lingual children's club – pre-school
☑ Multi-lingual children's club – 5-10 year olds
○ Multi-lingual children's club – 10-14 year olds
☑ Creative crafts
○ Bicycle hire for children
☑ Facilities for children in the wash blocks
○ Children's pool
☑ Children's play area
○ Crèche and/or babysitting
☑ Local information of interest for children

Facilities: Fourteen superb, fully equipped toilet blocks; 11 have facilities for disabled visitors. Launderette. Motorcaravan services. Gas supplies. Comprehensive shopping areas set around a pleasant piazza (all open till late). Eight restaurants each with a different style plus 11 pleasant and lively bars (all services open all season). Impressive aqua parks (all season). Tennis. Riding. Minigolf. Skating. Bicycle hire. Archery. Two fitness tracks in 4 ha. natural park with play area and supervised play. Golf academy. Diving centre and school. Windsurf school in season. Exhibitions. Boat excursions. Recreational events. Hairdressers. Internet cafés. ATM. Dogs are accepted in designated areas. WiFi over site (charged). Off site: Boat launching 3.5 km. Aqualandia (special rates). Excursions.

Open: 23 April - 27 September.

Directions: From Venice-Trieste autostrada leave at exit for airport or Quarto d'Altino and follow signs first for Jesolo and then Punta Sabbioni, and site will be seen just after Cavallino on the left.

GPS: 45.467883, 12.530367

Charges guide

Per unit incl. 2 persons and electricity	€ 19,80 - € 51,70
with services	€ 22,20 - € 70,90
extra person	€ 4,90 - € 12,20
child (1-11 yrs acc. to age)	€ 2,90 - € 9,90

Italy – *Cavallino-Treporti*

Camping Union Lido Vacanze

Via Fausta 258, I-30013 Cavallino-Treporti (Veneto)
t: 041 257 5111 e: info@unionlido.com
alanrogers.com/IT60200 www.unionlido.com

Accommodation: ✔ Pitch ✔ Mobile home/chalet ✔ Hotel/B&B ✔ Apartment

This amazing site is very large, offering absolutely everything a camper could wish for. It is extremely professionally run and we were impressed with the whole organisation. It lies along a 1.2 km. long, broad sandy beach which shelves very gradually and offers a huge number of sporting activities. The site itself is regularly laid out with parallel access roads under a covering of poplars, pine and other trees. There are 2,200 pitches for touring units, all with 6/10/16A electricity and 1,969 also have water and drainage. Because of the size of the site, there is an internal road train and amenities are repeated across the site. There are two aqua parks, one with fine sandy beaches and both have swimming pools, lagoon pools for children, a whirlpool and a 160 m. 'Wild River'. Another water park is planned. A huge selection of sports and activities are offered, and luxury amenities too numerous to list. Union Lido is, above all, an orderly and clean site. A member of Leading Campings group.

You might like to know

One of Europe's largest sites, looking straight out to the Adriatic with a long private beach (1,200 metres), Union Lido is a top quality holiday centre with a wide range of amenities.

- ✔ Multi-lingual children's club – pre-school
- ✔ Multi-lingual children's club – 5-10 year olds
- ✔ Multi-lingual children's club – 10-14 year olds
- ✔ Creative crafts
- ✔ Bicycle hire for children
- ✔ Facilities for children in the wash blocks
- ✔ Children's pool
- ✔ Children's play area
- ○ Crèche and/or babysitting
- ✔ Local information of interest for children

Facilities: Three toilet blocks are kept pristine and have hot water throughout. Facilities for disabled visitors. Washing machines. Large supermarket and shopping centre, bars, restaurants, cafés and pizzeria (all season; takeaway service 15/5-30/9). Excellent pool complex with slide and spa centre (all season). Tennis. Games room. Playground. Clubs for children. Entertainment programme. Direct beach access. Windsurf and pedalo hire. WiFi throughout (charged). Mobile homes, chalets and 14 eco-apartments for rent. Off site: ATM 500 m. Riding and boat launching 1 km. Golf and fishing 4 km. Walking and cycling trails. Excursions to Venice.

Open: 1 April - 30 September.

Directions: From A4 autostrada (approaching from Milan) take Mestre exit and follow signs initially for Venice airport and then Jesolo. From Jesolo, follow signs to Cavallino from where site is well signed.

GPS: 45.47380, 12.54903

Charges guide

Per unit incl. 2 persons and electricity	€ 20,00 - € 52,70
extra person	€ 5,00 - € 11,60
child (2-5 yrs)	€ 3,40 - € 10,20
dog	€ 2,70 - € 6,10

Camping Village Europa

Via Fausta 332, I-30013 Cavallino-Treporti (Veneto)
t: 041 968 069   e: info@campingeuropa.com
alanrogers.com/IT60410   www.campingeuropa.com

Accommodation: ☑ Pitch   ☑ Mobile home/chalet   ○ Hotel/B&B   ☑ Apartment

Europa is a smart, modern site in a great position with direct access to a fine, sandy, Blue Flag beach with lifeguards. There are 450 touring pitches, all with 8A electricity, water, drainage and satellite TV connections. The site is kept beautifully clean and neat and there is an impressive array of restaurants, bars, shops and leisure amenities. These are cleverly laid out along a central avenue and include a jeweller, a doctor's surgery, Internet services and much more. All manner of leisure facilities are arranged around the site. The touring area, with some great beachside pitches, is surprisingly peaceful for a site of this size. This site would be ideal for families. A professional team provides entertainment and regular themed summer events. Some restaurant tables have pleasant sea views. Venice is easily accessible by bus and then ferry from Punta Sabbioni.

You might like to know

Children are in safe hands at the miniclub, which has a wide range of activities organised by experienced entertainers.

- ☑ Multi-lingual children's club – pre-school
- ☑ Multi-lingual children's club – 5-10 year olds
- ○ Multi-lingual children's club – 10-14 year olds
- ☑ Creative crafts
- ○ Bicycle hire for children
- ○ Facilities for children in the wash blocks
- ☑ Children's pool
- ☑ Children's play area
- ○ Crèche and/or babysitting
- ○ Local information of interest for children

Camping Marina di Venezia

Via Montello 6, I-30013 Punta Sabbioni (Veneto)
t: 041 530 2511 e: camping@marinadivenezia.it
alanrogers.com/IT60450 www.marinadivenezia.it

Accommodation: ☑ Pitch ☑ Mobile home/chalet ○ Hotel/B&B ○ Apartment

This is an amazingly large site (2,915 pitches) with every conceivable facility. It has a pleasant feel, with cheerful staff and no notion of being overcrowded, even when full. Marina di Venezia has the advantage of being within walking distance of the ferry to Venice. It will appeal in particular to those who enjoy an extensive range of entertainment and activities and a lively atmosphere. Individual pitches are spacious and set on sandy or grassy ground; most are separated by trees or hedges. All are equipped with 10A electricity and water. The site's excellent sandy beach is one of the widest along this stretch of coast and has five pleasant beach bars. The 15,000 sq.m. wide, multi-level AquaMarina Park has exceptional facilities – a feature pool for children with slides and a huge cascade complex, an Olympic size pool with massage jets, a lagoon with disability access, and a wave pool with a beach. There are charming features for the youngest campers, a choice of whirlpool and a solarium on grass, plus an impressive 45-metre panoramic bridge.

Facilities: Nine modern toilet blocks are maintained to a very high standard with hot showers and a high proportion of British style toilets. Pleasant facilities for disabled visitors. Laundry. Range of shops. Several bars, restaurants and takeaways. Five beach bars/snack bars. Enormous swimming pool complex with slides and flumes. Several play areas. Tennis. Surfboard and catamaran hire. Wide range of organised entertainment. WiFi (charged). Special area and facilities for dog owners (also beach area). Off site: Fishing 1 km. Riding 7 km. Golf 10 km.

Open: 12 April - 30 September.

Directions: From A4 motorway, take Jesolo exit. After Jesolo continue towards Punta Sabbioni. Site is clearly signed to the left towards the end of this road, close to the Venice ferries.

GPS: 45.43750, 12.43805

Charges guide

Per unit incl. 2 persons and electricity	€ 21,10 - € 48,50
extra person	€ 4,70 - € 10,90
child or senior (2-5 and over 60)	€ 3,90 - € 8,70
dog	€ 1,50 - € 5,10

You might like to know

There's plenty to keep the children busy: Gommaland, Leo Golf, baby cars, bumper boats and a playground. In high season, the entertainment programme offers dance, workshops, games, sport tournaments and ballet school.

- ☑ Multi-lingual children's club – pre-school
- ☑ Multi-lingual children's club – 5-10 year olds
- ☑ Multi-lingual children's club – 10-14 year olds
- ☑ Creative crafts
- ☑ Bicycle hire for children
- ☑ Facilities for children in the wash blocks
- ☑ Children's pool
- ☑ Children's play area
- ○ Crèche and/or babysitting
- ○ Local information of interest for children

Camping Residence Corones

Niederrasen 124, I-39030 Rasen (Trentino - Alto Adige)
t: 047 449 6490 e: info@corones.com
alanrogers.com/IT61990 www.corones.com

Accommodation: ☑ Pitch ☑ Mobile home/chalet ○ Hotel/B&B ☑ Apartment

Situated in a pine forest clearing at the foot of the attractive Antholz valley in the heart of German-speaking Südtirol, Corones is ideally situated both for winter sports enthusiasts and for walkers, cyclists, mountain bikers and those who prefer to explore the valleys and mountain roads of the Dolomites by car. There are 135 level pitches, all with 16A electricity and many also with water, drainage and satellite TV. The Residence offers luxury apartments and there are authentic Canadian log cabins for hire. The bar/restaurant and small shop are open all season. From the site you can see slopes which in winter become highly rated skiing pistes. A short drive up the broad Antholz/Anterselva valley takes you to an internationally important biathlon centre. An excellent day trip would be to drive up the valley and over the pass into Austria and then back via another pass. Back on site, a small pool and paddling pool could be very welcome.

You might like to know

The miniclub has a weekly programme, including arts and crafts, forest activities, fun in the pool, and family excursions.

○ Multi-lingual children's club – pre-school
☑ Multi-lingual children's club – 5-10 year olds
○ Multi-lingual children's club – 10-14 year olds
☑ Creative crafts
○ Bicycle hire for children
☑ Facilities for children in the wash blocks
☑ Children's pool
☑ Children's play area
☑ Crèche and/or babysitting
○ Local information of interest for children

Facilities: The central toilet block is traditional but well maintained and clean. Additional facilities below the Residence are of the highest quality including individual shower rooms with washbasins, washbasins with all WCs, a delightful children's unit and an excellent facility for disabled visitors. Fully equipped private shower rooms for hire. Luxurious wellness centre with saunas, solarium, jacuzzis, massage, therapy pools and heat benches. Heated outdoor swimming and paddling pools (4/5-20/10). Play area. WiFi throughout (charged). Charcoal barbecues are not permitted. Off site: Tennis 800 m. Bicycle hire 1 km. Riding and fishing 3 km. Golf (9 holes) 10 km. Canoeing/kayaking 15 km.

Open: 6 December - 7 April,
9 May - 27 October.

Directions: Rasen/Rasun is 85 km. northeast of Bolzano. From Bressanone/Brixen exit on A22 Brenner-Modena motorway, go east on SS49 for 50 km. then turn north (signed Rasen/Antholz). Turn immediately west at roundabout in Niederrasen/Rasun di Sotto to site on left in 100 m.

GPS: 46.7758, 12.0367

Charges guide

Per unit incl. 2 persons, electricity on meter	€ 23,50 - € 33,80
extra person	€ 5,70 - € 8,90
child (3-15 yrs)	€ 3,20 - € 8,00
dog	€ 2,50 - € 4,50

No credit cards.

Camping Seiser Alm

Saint Konstantin 16, I-39050 Völs am Schlern (Trentino - Alto Adige)
t: 047 170 6459   e: info@camping-seiseralm.com
alanrogers.com/IT62040   www.camping-seiseralm.com

Accommodation: ☑ Pitch   ☑ Mobile home/chalet   ○ Hotel/B&B   ☑ Apartment

Facilities: One spotless, luxury underground block is in the centre of the site. 16 private units are available. Excellent facilities for disabled visitors. Fairy tale facilities for children. Infrared sensors, underfloor heating and gently curved floors to prevent slippery surfaces. Laundry facilities. Sauna. Supermarket. Quality restaurant and bar with terrace. Swimming pool (heated in cool weather). Entertainment programme. Miniclub. Children's adventure park and play room. Rooms for ski equipment. Animal enclosure. WiFi (charged). Apartments, mobile homes and maxi-caravans for rent. Off site: Riding alongside site. 18-hole golf course (discounts) and fishing 1 km. Bicycle hire and lake swimming 2 km. ATM 3 km. Paragilding. Mountain biking. Walking. Skiing in winter. Buses to cable cars and ski lifts.

Open: All year excl. 2 November - 20 December.

Directions: From A22-E45 take Bolzano Nord exit. Take road for Prato Isarco/Blumau, then road for Fie/Völs. Road divides suddenly – if you miss the left fork as you enter a tunnel (Altopiano dello Sciliar/Schlerngebiet) you will pay a heavy price in extra kilometres. Enjoy the climb to Völs am Schlern and site is well signed.

GPS: 46.53344, 11.53335

Charges guide

Per unit incl. 2 persons	€ 19,60 - € 47,00
extra person	€ 7,30 - € 10,50
child (2-16 yrs)	€ 3,60 - € 8,30
electricity (per kWh)	€ 0,60
dog	€ 3,50 - € 5,20

What an amazing experience awaits you at Seiser Alm! Elisabeth and Erhard Mahlknecht have created a superb site in the magnificent Südtirol region of the Dolomite mountains. Towering peaks provide a wonderful backdrop when you dine in the charming, traditionally styled restaurant on the upper terrace. The 165 touring pitches (with 16A electricity), 150 with gas, water, drainage, satellite connection and WiFi. Guests were delighted with the site when we visited, many coming to walk or cycle, some just to enjoy the surroundings. There are countless things to see and do here, including a full entertainment programme and a brilliant new pool. Enjoy the grand 18-hole golf course alongside the site or join the organised excursions and activities. Local buses and cable cars provide an excellent service for summer visitors and skiers alike. In keeping with the natural setting, the majority of the luxury facilities are set into the hillside. A family play park with an enclosure of animals is at the lower part of the site where goats also roam. If you wish for quiet, quality camping in a crystal clean environment, then visit this immaculate site.

You might like to know

In the lower part of the site is a small animal park with tame rabbits and goats.

○ Multi-lingual children's club – pre-school
☑ Multi-lingual children's club – 5-10 year olds
☑ Multi-lingual children's club – 10-14 year olds
☑ Creative crafts
○ Bicycle hire for children
☑ Facilities for children in the wash blocks
○ Children's pool
☑ Children's play area
☑ Crèche and/or babysitting
☑ Local information of interest for children

Italy – Laives/Leifers

Camping-Park Steiner

J. F. Kennedy Str. 32, I-39055 Laives/Leifers (Trentino - Alto Adige)
t: 047 195 0105   e: info@campingsteiner.com
alanrogers.com/IT62100   www.campingsteiner.com

Accommodation: ☑ Pitch   ☑ Mobile home/chalet   ☑ Hotel/B&B   ○ Apartment

The very welcoming Camping Steiner is very central for touring with the whole of the Dolomite region within easy reach. With a happy atmosphere and much on-site activity, one could spend an enjoyable holiday here. The 180 individual touring pitches, mostly with good shade and hardstanding, are in rows with easy access and all have 6A electricity. There is a pleasant, family style pizzeria/restaurant with a great menu, plus indoor and outdoor pools with a sunbathing area. The Steiner Park Hotel at the entrance to the site provides another restaurant, café and full hotel facilities. This friendly, family run site has a long tradition of providing a happy camping experience in the more traditional style – the owner remembers Alan Rogers who stayed here on many occasions. It is easy to get to different parts of the Dolomites which is ideal for walkers. There are also 30 chalets available to rent located to one side of the site.

You might like to know

There is a choice of lake beaches within the area, special events and much more.

- ○ Multi-lingual children's club – pre-school
- ○ Multi-lingual children's club – 5-10 year olds
- ○ Multi-lingual children's club – 10-14 year olds
- ○ Creative crafts
- ☑ Bicycle hire for children
- ☑ Facilities for children in the wash blocks
- ☑ Children's pool
- ☑ Children's play area
- ○ Crèche and/or babysitting
- ☑ Local information of interest for children

Facilities: The two sanitary blocks are equipped to a high standard. They can be heated in cool weather. Facilities for disabled campers. Shop. Bar/pizzeria/restaurant with takeaway (11/4-30/10). Outdoor pool with paddling pool (11/4-30/9). Aquagym. Smaller covered heated pool (11/4-30/10). Playground. Entertainment incl. wine tastings. Dogs are not accepted in July/Aug. WiFi in some areas (free). Off site: Bicycle hire 300 m. Fishing 2.5 km. Riding 3 km. Bozen/Bolzano 8 km. wirth bus service from outside site.

Open: 21 March - 31 October.

Directions: Site is by the SS12 on northern edge of Leifers, 8 km. south of Bolzano. If approaching from north, at the Bolzano-Süd exit from A22 Brenner-Modena motorway follow Trento signs for 7 km. then signs for 'centre' Leifers/Laives. From south on motorway take Ora exit, then north on SS12 towards Bolzano for 14 km. then signs for 'centre' Leifers/Laives.

GPS: 46.42950, 11.3434

Charges guide

Per unit incl. 2 persons and electricity	€ 28,00 - € 36,00
extra person	€ 7,00 - € 9,00
child (under 9 yrs)	€ 4,00 - € 6,00

Less 10% for 2 weeks or more.

Facilities: Two very clean and modern sanitary blocks near reception have British and Turkish style WCs and hot water throughout. Laundry. Motorcaravan services. Combined restaurant/bar/pizzeria/takeaway and shop. A swimming pool and paddling pool (1/4-31/10) and private beach. Tennis. Volleyball. Excellent play area. Wood-burning stove and barbecue. Fishing. Diving. Entertainment for children and adults in high season. Excursions. Bicycle hire. WiFi over site. Off site: Supermarket 200 m. Bus 200 m. Aquapark 500 m. Riding and golf 2 km. Ancient town of Albenga (2,000 years old) 3 km. Parachuting school 10 km. Local markets.

Open: 1 April - 20 October, 4 December - 10 January.

Directions: From the A10 between Imperia and Savona, take Albenga exit. Follow signs Ceriale/Savona and Aquapark Caravelle (which is 500 m. from site) and then site signs. Site is just south of Savona.

GPS: 44.08165, 8.21763

Charges guide

Per unit incl. up to 3 persons (over 2 yrs) and electricity	€ 23,00 - € 51,00
extra person	€ 6,50 - € 11,00
dog	€ 3,00 - € 5,00

Discounts for stays in excess of 7 days.

Italy – Ceriale

Camping Baciccia

Via Torino 19, I-17023 Ceriale (Ligúria)
t: 018 299 0743 e: info@campingbaciccia.it
alanrogers.com/IT64030 www.campingbaciccia.it

Accommodation: ☑ Pitch ☑ Mobile home/chalet ○ Hotel/B&B ○ Apartment

This friendly, family run site is a popular holiday destination. Baciccia was the nickname of the present owner's grandfather who grew fruit trees and tomatoes on the site. Tall eucalyptus trees shade the 106 flat touring pitches. Laura and Mauro work tirelessly to ensure that you enjoy your stay here and we have watched the growth of a very effective campsite over the years. An informal restaurant, overlooking the swimming pool and sports area, is cheerfully and efficiently run by Flavio and Pamela who serve delightful seasonal Italian dishes. The pool has a giant elephant slide which is always busy. There is a free shuttle to the site's private beach and the town has the usual seaside attractions. This site will suit campers looking for a family atmosphere with none of the brashness of large seaside sites. If you have forgotten anything by way of camping equipment just ask and the family will probably be able to lend it to you.

You might like to know

There is plenty to do off site: a free beach and a water park (both 500 m), and a fascinating aquarium (in Genoa, 80 km).

○ Multi-lingual children's club – pre-school
○ Multi-lingual children's club – 5-10 year olds
○ Multi-lingual children's club – 10-14 year olds
☑ Creative crafts
○ Bicycle hire for children
○ Facilities for children in the wash blocks
☑ Children's pool
☑ Children's play area
○ Crèche and/or babysitting
☑ Local information of interest for children

Facilities:
Facilities: Three sanitary blocks with free hot showers. Facilities for disabled visitors. Motorcaravan services. Laundry. Bar. Restaurant. Takeaway. Pizzeria. Shop. Swimming pools (hats must be worn) with solarium terrace. Play area and sports ground. Tennis. Bowling. WiFi (charged). Bicycle hire. Entertainment in high season. Clubs for children and teenagers. Pets are allowed only on assigned pitches. Bungalows to rent. Off site: Beach. Canoe and pedalo hire.

Open: 1 May - 18 October.

Directions: From north or south on A14 motorway, take exit Roseto degli Abruzzi exit. Turn onto SS150 to Roseto degli Abruzzi. Pass under 4 m. bridge below railway at south end of town, and right onto coast road. From Rome and L'Aquila on A24 motorway take Villa Vomano-Teramo exit onto SS150 (Roseto degli Abruzzi).

GPS: 42.6577, 14.0353

Charges guide

Per unit incl. 2 persons and electricity € 18,00 - € 42,50	
extra person € 4,50 - € 11,00	
child (4-9 yrs) € 3,00 - € 7,00	
dog € 4,00 - € 5,00	

Italy – Roseto degli Abruzzi

Camping Village Eurcamping

Lungomare Trieste Sud, I-64026 Roseto degli Abruzzi (Abruzzo)
t: 085 899 3179 e: eurcamping@camping.it
alanrogers.com/IT68040 www.eurcamping.it

Accommodation: ☑ Pitch ☑ Mobile home/chalet ○ Hotel/B&B ○ Apartment

Eurcamping is about 2 km. south of the small town of Roseto degli Abruzzi, at the end of the coastal road which runs parallel to the SS16. This is a relatively quiet site, situated beside the sea, but with no direct access to it. There are 265 well defined pitches, many under green screens, and all with 3/6A electricity. Accessing the site is not difficult, but you have to pass under the coastal railway line so must use the bridge with 4 m. headroom. There is some road noise but little from the railway. There are good facilities including an outdoor fitness course, an entertainment area at the far end of the site and a pleasant swimming pool just inside the entrance. Some entertainment is provided for children in high season. There is a small harbour and yacht club nearby and a small sandy section of the beach about 75 m. away with sun shades and loungers. This is solely for the use of visitors to the campsite.

You might like to know

Children up to the age of 4 go free!

○ Multi-lingual children's club – pre-school
☑ Multi-lingual children's club – 5-10 year olds
☑ Multi-lingual children's club – 10-14 year olds
☑ Creative crafts
☑ Bicycle hire for children
○ Facilities for children in the wash blocks
☑ Children's pool
☑ Children's play area
○ Crèche and/or babysitting
☑ Local information of interest for children

Facilities: Laundry. Shop. Café/bar. Restaurant and pizzeria. Rental accommodation. Bicycle hire. WiFi. Off site: Riding 100 m. Boat trips and hire. Fishing. Steam train. Archaeological sites.

Open: 1 April - 15 October.

Directions: Camping La Pineta is 80 km. northeast of Cagliari. From Cagliari take SS125 towards Olbia. Just after Tertenia follow signs to Barisardo. On entering Barisardo follow signs on right to site in 3 km.

GPS: 39.82028, 9.67032

Charges guide

Per unit incl. 2 persons and electricity € 15,00 - € 33,50	
extra person € 4,00 - € 9,00	
child (3-10 yrs) € 2,50 - € 6,00	
dog no charge	

Italy – Bari Sardo

Camping La Pineta

Localitá Planargia, I-08042 Bari Sardo (Sardinia)
t: 078 229 372 e: info@campingbungalowlapineta.it
alanrogers.com/IT69715 www.campingbungalowlapineta.it

Accommodation: ☑ Pitch ☑ Mobile home/chalet ○ Hotel/B&B ○ Apartment

Camping La Pineta is a small, family run campsite on the island of Sardinia. It lies just 400 metres from the clean, safe, Mediterranean beach of Planargia. Set amongst mature pine and eucalyptus trees this 1.5-hectare campsite has a mixture of mobile homes and shaded touring pitches, some of which are suitable for tents, others can accommodate caravans or motorcaravans. All have electricity points and water close by. The restaurant, café/bar, pizzeria and mini-market cater for most needs, whilst the small town of Barisardo (3.5 kilometres) has a wider range of amenities. The staff will assist with ferry and flight bookings if required. La Pineta is in a quiet, rural location but would make a good base for exploring the varied coastline and Saracen towers. A short distance inland, you are in the mountainous areas with a multitude of geologically interesting natural formations. Many places can be reached by foot, by mountain bike or even on horseback. The nearby little green steam train will take you through some stunning scenery on its unspoilt route through the hills.

You might like to know

Nearby diving schools offer diving and snorkelling for children.

- ○ Multi-lingual children's club – pre-school
- ○ Multi-lingual children's club – 5-10 year olds
- ○ Multi-lingual children's club – 10-14 year olds
- ○ Creative crafts
- ☑ Bicycle hire for children
- ○ Facilities for children in the wash blocks
- ○ Children's pool
- ☑ Children's play area
- ○ Crèche and/or babysitting
- ○ Local information of interest for children

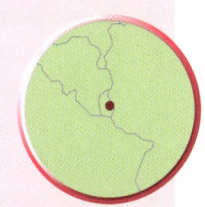

Facilities:
Facilities: Three modern heated sanitary buildings well situated around the site include mostly open washbasins (6 cabins in one block). Baby baths. Facilities (including accommodation to rent) for wheelchair users. Washing machines and dryers. Motorcaravan services. Shops. Coffee bar. Restaurant with terrace. Swimming pool with sliding cupola (heated 15/5-15/9). Outdoor pool for toddlers. Sauna. Play areas. Trampolines. Volleyball. Minigolf. Tennis. Bicycle hire. Riding. Internet points. Free WiFi over site. Off site: Golf 5 km. Fishing and kayaking 10 km.

Open: 16 March - 3 November.

Directions: From N7 (Diekirch-Luxembourg City), turn onto N8 (CR118) at Berschbach (just past Mersch) towards Larochette. Site is signed on the right 1.5 km. from Larochette. Approach road is fairly steep and narrow.

GPS: 49.78508, 6.21033

Charges guide

Per unit incl. 2 persons and electricity	€ 19,50 - € 36,00
with water and drainage	€ 22,50 - € 39,00
extra person	€ 4,25
dog	€ 2,50

Camping Birkelt

1 Um Birkelt, L-7633 Larochette (Luxembourg)
t: 879 040   e: info@camping-birkelt.lu
alanrogers.com/LU7610   www.camping-birkelt.lu

Accommodation: ☑ Pitch   ☑ Mobile home/chalet   ◯ Hotel/B&B   ◯ Apartment

This is very much a family site, with a great range of facilities provided. It is well organised and well laid out, set in an elevated position in attractive, undulating countryside. A tarmac road runs around the site with 427 large grass pitches (280 for touring), some slightly sloping, many with a fair amount of shade, on either side of gravel access roads in straight rows and circles. Two hundred pitches have electricity, 134 serviced ones have 16A, the remainder 10A. An all-weather swimming pool complex is beside the site entrance (free for campers) and entertainment for children is arranged in high season. The site is very popular with tour operators (140 pitches). The main activities take place adjacent to the large, circular, all-weather family pool. This is an outdoor pool in high season and covered and heated in cooler weather. Several play areas are dotted all over the site. The site entrance has been made vehicle free (vehicle entrance is on a separate road) and provides a pleasant terrace and shopping area. Seven serviced, overnight motorcaravan pitches are provided in the car park area. Throughout the site, all signage is in four languages including English.

You might like to know

Müllerthal is well known for its forests and medieval castles, such as Larochette and Beaufort. A visit is highly recommended.

☑ Multi-lingual children's club – pre-school
☑ Multi-lingual children's club – 5-10 year olds
☑ Multi-lingual children's club – 10-14 year olds
☑ Creative crafts
◯ Bicycle hire for children
☑ Facilities for children in the wash blocks
☑ Children's pool
☑ Children's play area
◯ Crèche and/or babysitting
☑ Local information of interest for children

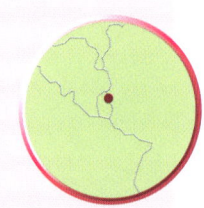

Facilities

Facilities: Heated sanitary block with showers and washbasins in cabins. Facilities for disabled visitors. Motorcaravan services. Laundry. Bar, restaurant, takeaway (open all season). Baker calls daily. Games/TV room. Sports field with play equipment. Boules. Bicycle hire. Golf weeks. Discounts on six local 18-hole golf courses. WiFi over site. Apartments to rent. Off site: Bus to Clervaux and Vianden stops (4 times daily) outside site entrance. Riding 5 km. Castle at Vianden 14 km. Monastery at Clervaux 14 km. Golf 15 km.

Open: 11 April - 4 November.

Directions: Take N7 north from Diekirch. At Hosingen, turn right onto the narrow and winding CR324 signed Eisenbach. Follow site signs from Eisenbach or Obereisenbach.

GPS: 50.01602, 6.13600

Charges guide

Per unit incl. 2 persons
and electricity € 19,90 - € 28,00

extra person € 5,00

dog € 3,00

Luxembourg – Eisenbach

Camping Kohnenhof

Kounenhaff 1, L-9838 Eisenbach (Luxembourg)
t: 929 464 e: kohnenhof@pt.lu
alanrogers.com/LU7680 www.campingkohnenhof.lu

Accommodation: ☑ Pitch ☑ Mobile home/chalet ○ Hotel/B&B ☑ Apartment

Nestling in a valley with the River Our running through it, Camping Kohnenhof offers a very agreeable location for a relaxing family holiday. From the minute you stop at the reception you are assured of a warm and friendly welcome. There are 105 pitches, 80 for touring, all with 6/16A electricity. Numerous paths cross through the wooded hillside so this could be a haven for walkers. A little bridge crosses the small river over the border to Germany. The river is shallow and safe for children (parental supervision essential). A large sports field and play area with a selection of equipment caters for younger campers. During the high season, an entertainment programme is organised for parents and children. The owner organises special golf weeks with games on different courses and discounts have been agreed at several local courses (contact the site for details). The restaurant is part of an old farmhouse and offers a wonderful ambience to enjoy a meal.

You might like to know

Kohnenhof is well known for its river, where customers can enjoy some relaxing fishing (permits sold at reception).

☑ Multi-lingual children's club – pre-school
☑ Multi-lingual children's club – 5-10 year olds
☑ Multi-lingual children's club – 10-14 year olds
☑ Creative crafts
☑ Bicycle hire for children
○ Facilities for children in the wash blocks
☑ Children's pool
☑ Children's play area
○ Crèche and/or babysitting
○ Local information of interest for children

Facilities: Two very clean and well appointed sanitary blocks include some washbasins in cabins and facilities for children. Toilet and shower facilities for disabled visitors and for babies. Laundry facilities. Motorcaravan services. Bar/restaurant with terrace and large TVs and LCD projection. Snack bar. Heated outdoor swimming pool (15/5-15/9). Playground. Bicycle hire. Pool tables. Sports field. Entertainment for children and teenagers. WiFi (free).
Off site: Tennis and watersports nearby. Riding 1 km. Shop 800 m. Fishing 2.5 km.

Open: 1 April - 27 October.

Directions: Site is west of the village of Kamperland on the island of Noord Beveland. From the N256 Goes-Zierikzee road, exit west onto the N255 Kamperland road. Site is signed south of this road.

GPS: 51.57840, 3.69642

Charges guide

Per unit incl. 2 persons
and electricity € 21,00 - € 34,00

extra person € 2,00 - € 3,50

dog € 4,00 - € 5,00

Netherlands – Kamperland

Camping De Molenhoek

Molenweg 69a, NL-4493 NC Kamperland (Zeeland)
t: 0113 371 202 e: info@demolenhoek.com
alanrogers.com/NL5570 www.demolenhoek.com

Accommodation: ☑ Pitch ☑ Mobile home/chalet ○ Hotel/B&B ○ Apartment

This rural, family run site makes a pleasant contrast to the livelier coastal sites in this popular holiday area. There is an emphasis on catering for the users of the 300 permanent or seasonal holiday caravans and 100 tourers. Eighty of these have 6A electricity, water and drainage. The site is neat and tidy with surrounding hedges and trees giving privacy and some shade, and electrical connections are available. A large outdoor pool area has ample space for swimming, children's play and sun loungers. Entertainment, including dance evenings and bingo, is organised in season. Although the site is quietly situated, there are many excursion possibilities in the area including the towns of Middelburg, Veere and Goes and the Delta Expo exhibition, which includes a waterpark, Neeltje Jans. It is close to Veerse Meer, which is very popular with watersports enthusiasts. The surrounding area has many beaches set among the dune landscape, and these are easily reached by car or bicycle.

You might like to know

The unique Kids & Co entertainment programme runs on Ascension Day, Whitsun and in July and August. It's free for all guests, and great fun for kids and parents alike.

- ☑ Multi-lingual children's club – pre-school
- ☑ Multi-lingual children's club – 5-10 year olds
- ☑ Multi-lingual children's club – 10-14 year olds
- ☑ Creative crafts
- ☑ Bicycle hire for children
- ☑ Facilities for children in the wash blocks
- ☑ Children's pool
- ☑ Children's play area
- ○ Crèche and/or babysitting
- ☑ Local information of interest for children

Camping Meerwijck

Strandweg 2, NL-9606 PR Kropswolde (Groningen)
t: 0598 323 659 e: info@meerwijck.nl
alanrogers.com/NL5775 www.meerwijck.nl

Accommodation: ☑ Pitch ☑ Mobile home/chalet ○ Hotel/B&B ○ Apartment

This large lakeside site (23 hectares) has 500 pitches (200 for touring units) and is beautifully located on the beaches of the Zuidlaardermeer. The touring pitches are arranged on several separate fields away from the mobile homes and seasonal guests, either in circular bays or in long rows from paved access lanes. All touring pitches have electricity (6A), water, waste water and cable TV connections. This site is ideal for youngsters as there is direct access to the sandy beaches and there is an indoor heated swimming pool with a paddling pool. In high season an entertainment team provides games and excursions for youngsters and adults. Camping Meerwijck is a useful base from which to explore the surroundings of the province of Groningen and the bustling Hanseatic city itself is only 20 km. away and easily accessible by bicycle. The site has its own marina for 215 small sailing boats and motor boats and there is a slipway. Meerwijck is in a small nature reserve, which offers good opportunities for walking and cycling. Villages such as Hoogezand and Zuidlaren are nearby, with good opportunities for shopping, including local markets.

You might like to know

In lovely natural surroundings, the site and marina are located at the beautiful Zuidlaardermeer Meerwijck. There is a lovely sandy beach and forest playgrounds.

- ☑ Multi-lingual children's club – pre-school
- ☑ Multi-lingual children's club – 5-10 year olds
- ☑ Multi-lingual children's club – 10-14 year olds
- ☑ Creative crafts
- ☑ Bicycle hire for children
- ☑ Facilities for children in the wash blocks
- ☑ Children's pool
- ☑ Children's play area
- ○ Crèche and/or babysitting
- ☑ Local information of interest for children

Facilities: Three modern and clean toilet blocks for touring units with hot showers (six minutes), washbasins (open style and in cabins), family bathrooms, baby rooms and facilities for disabled visitors. Laundry facilities. Small supermarket. Bar and snack bar. Indoor pool (15x20 m) with paddling pool. Playing field. Multisports court. Playgrounds. Animal farm. Tennis. Fishing. Bicycle hire. Marina. Activity team in high season. Lake with sandy beaches. WiFi throughout (charged). Off site: Restaurant at the beach. Riding 3 km. Golf 10 km. Hoogezand 2 km. Zuidlaren 10 km.

Open: 30 March - 29 September.

Directions: On A7 to and from Groningen, take exit for Foxhol and continue south towards Kropswolde. Cross the canal and the railway and turn right at next roundabout towards site.

GPS: 53.14316, 6.68916

Charges guide

Per unit incl. 2 persons and electricity € 20,00 - € 27,00	
extra person € 4,00	
boat trailer € 2,50	
dog € 3,00	

Facilities
Facilities: Several toilet blocks are well placed around the site, with washbasins in cabins and hot showers. Laundry. Shop. Bar and snack bar/restaurant with open-air terrace. Heated indoor and outdoor pool complex and spa centre. Multisports court. Bicycle hire. Indoor playground and theatre. Playgrounds. WiFi over site (charged). Full entertainment team in season and school holidays. Dogs only allowed on some fields. Off site: The sand dunes, forests, juniper fields and the Vecht river of Overijssel provide opportunities for day trips.

Open: April - November (accommodation all year).

Directions: From A28, take exit 21 (Ommen) and continue east towards Ommen. From Ommen, follow N34 northeast and turn south on N36 at crossing. Site is signed from there.

GPS: 52.51139, 6.54618

Charges guide
Per unit incl. 2 persons
and full service pitch € 23,00 - € 45,30

extra person € 4,00 - € 5,20

dog € 3,50

Netherlands – Ommen

Vrijetijdspark Beerze Bulten

Kampweg 1, NL-7736 PK Beerze-Ommen (Overijssel)
t: 0523 251 398 e: info@beerzebulten.nl
alanrogers.com/NL5985 www.beerzebulten.nl

Accommodation: ✔ Pitch ✔ Mobile home/chalet ○ Hotel/B&B ○ Apartment

Beerze Bulten is a large leisure park with superb indoor and outdoor amenities, so you can enjoy yourself whatever the weather. A large, partly underground 'rabbit hole' provides a big indoor playground for children, a theatre for both indoor and outdoor shows, a buffet, a superb full wellness spa and a very large, specially designed indoor pool. Beerze Bulten has 550 pitches, mainly for touring units, but also accommodation for hire (all year). In the shade of mature woodland, all the pitches are level and numbered, and all have 10A Europlug electricity, water, drainage and TV connections. To the rear of the site is a large lake area with a sandy beach and new, exciting adventure play equipment. As well as heated indoor and outdoor pools, a fun paddling pool, jet stream, several different saunas and a water playground, this also offers full fitness facilities and a special salt cave treatment for those suffering from asthma or skin troubles. The snack bar/restaurant and terrace are very popular. Beerze Bulten will provide a relaxing and active family holiday.

You might like to know

Look forward to spectacular shows, great musicals and lots of fun in the Giant Rabbit Hole playground, home of Bultje the bunny. The fun-filled entertainment includes original songs, specially written for Beerze Bulten.

- ✔ Multi-lingual children's club – pre-school
- ✔ Multi-lingual children's club – 5-10 year olds
- ✔ Multi-lingual children's club – 10-14 year olds
- ✔ Creative crafts
- ✔ Bicycle hire for children
- ✔ Facilities for children in the wash blocks
- ✔ Children's pool
- ✔ Children's play area
- ○ Crèche and/or babysitting
- ✔ Local information of interest for children

Netherlands – Emst-Gortel

Camping De Wildhoeve

Hanendorperweg 102, NL-8166 JJ Emst-Gortel (Gelderland)
t: 0578 661 324 e: info@wildhoeve.nl
alanrogers.com/NL6285 www.wildhoeve.nl

Accommodation: ☑ Pitch ☑ Mobile home/chalet ○ Hotel/B&B ○ Apartment

Camping De Wildhoeve is an exceptional, welcoming, privately owned site with many amenities of the type one would normally find on larger holiday camps. The well maintained site is located in woodland and has 400 pitches with 330 for tourers. Pitching is in several areas, mostly in the shade of mature conifers. Partly separated by trees and bushes, the level pitches are numbered and all have 6/10A electricity, water and drainage. Behind reception is an octagonal-shaped, indoor sub-tropical pool with a large water slide and fun paddling pool. Next to reception is a water adventure playground with a small beach. To the front of the site are tennis courts and next to that is another open-air pool with a large slide. Here also is a shop plus a grand café/restaurant with terrace. Many activities are organised for children, including open-air theatre. The toilet facilities on this site are excellent and include a block with a special area for children with disabilities.

You might like to know

With the Camping Wildhoeve as a starting point, you can join a gamekeeper, who will show you the secrets of nature. You may also join a nature photographer, who will teach you how to take the best nature photographs.

- ○ Multi-lingual children's club – pre-school
- ☑ Multi-lingual children's club – 5-10 year olds
- ☑ Multi-lingual children's club – 10-14 year olds
- ☑ Creative crafts
- ○ Bicycle hire for children
- ☑ Facilities for children in the wash blocks
- ☑ Children's pool
- ☑ Children's play area
- ○ Crèche and/or babysitting
- ☑ Local information of interest for children

Facilities: Four well placed, heated blocks with toilets, washbasins (open style and in cabins) and free, preset hot showers. Special section for children with showers, washbasins and toilets. Baby room. Family shower room. Facilities for disabled children. Laundry facilities. Shop, grand café/restaurant. Snack bar. Indoor and outdoor pools with slides and paddling pool. Water adventure playground. Bicycle hire. Tennis. Open-air theatre. WiFi over site (charged). Dogs are not accepted. Off site: Fishing 4 km. Riding 5 km. Paleis Het Loo. Apeldoorn. Wild Animal Park, Wissel.

Open: April - September.

Directions: From the A28, take exit 15 (Epe/Nunspeet). Continue east towards Epe and at traffic lights turn south towards Emst. Continue straight ahead at roundabout in Emst. Turn right at church, into Hanendorperweg. Site is on the right after 3.5 km.

GPS: 52.31369, 5.92707

Charges guide

Per unit incl. 2 persons
and electricity € 21,00 - € 37,75

extra person € 5,00

Facilities: Three toilet blocks are conveniently situated around the touring areas. En-suite unit for disabled campers. Laundry. Well stocked shop. Bar with TV. Restaurant. Snack bar/takeaway. Heated indoor pool. Play area. Entertainment for younger children (high season). Bicycle hire. WiFi over site. Accommodation for hire. Max. 1 dog per pitch. Off site: Golf 3 km. Fishing and riding 10 km.

Open: 27 March - 24 October.

Directions: From the A1 between Amersfoort and Apeldoorn, take exit 16 N303 to Voorthuizen then onto the N344 towards Garderen. The site is signed soon after leaving Voorthuizen.

GPS: 52.18692, 5.62458

Charges guide

Per unit incl. 2 persons
and electricity € 22,50 - € 36,50

| extra person € 5,00 |
| dog (max. 1) € 5,00 |

Recreatiecentrum Ackersate

Harremaatweg 26, NL-3781 NJ Voorthuizen (Gelderland)
t: 0342 471 274 e: ackersate@ardoer.com
alanrogers.com/NL6336 www.ardoer.com

Accommodation: ☑ Pitch   ☑ Mobile home/chalet   ○ Hotel/B&B   ○ Apartment

This is a sophisticated, wooded site with 150 touring pitches out of a total of 490, all with 6/10A electricity. The swimming pool has a fun pool with slides, a large pool for young children, imaginatively designed, a separate pool for length swimming and even a flume. Also popular, is the cosy restaurant/bar. There is a play club for children, a playing field and a petting farm. Other activities available include minigolf, table tennis and a pool table. Active visitors might enjoy a game of volleyball or football. Voorthuizen is the small town close to the site, while Amersfoort, Apeldoorn, The Kröller-Müller Museum (a large collection of Van Gogh paintings), and the Hoge Veluwe National Park are all easily visited by car. Just 1 km. away is Recreatieplas Zeumeren, a large lake with a sandy beach and wealth of facilities – ideal for a picnic or just a stroll around the lake. You will also find SchatEiland there, which has plenty of entertainment for children. The friendly, helpful reception will be pleased to tell you about all that the surrounding area has to offer. A member of the Ardoer Group.

You might like to know

There is an entertainment team on site during the school holidays.

- ☑ Multi-lingual children's club – pre-school
- ☑ Multi-lingual children's club – 5-10 year olds
- ☑ Multi-lingual children's club – 10-14 year olds
- ○ Creative crafts
- ☑ Bicycle hire for children
- ☑ Facilities for children in the wash blocks
- ☑ Children's pool
- ☑ Children's play area
- ○ Crèche and/or babysitting
- ☑ Local information of interest for children

Recreatiepark De Boshoek

Harremaatweg 34, NL-3781 NJ Voorthuizen (Gelderland)
t: 0342 471 297 e: info@deboshoek.nl
alanrogers.com/NL6337 www.deboshoek.nl

Accommodation: ☑ Pitch ○ Mobile home/chalet ☑ Hotel/B&B ○ Apartment

Camping de Boshoek is a spacious, family oriented campsite, which forms a part of a large leisure park which includes bungalows for rent and private chalets. There are 130 touring pitches of 100-120 sq.m, all equipped with 10A electricity, water, drainage and cable TV connections. They are in various fields, each with its own play area and including two car-free areas, with a central area for general use. There are eight pitches reserved for campers. Rented accommodation includes comfortable safari tents equipped with kitchen, terrace and a private bathroom. Children will enjoy the playground with its giant 7.5-metre slide. There is also a pony club and a children's farm. The sports park includes an interactive soccer wall and many other amenities for all age groups, including minigolf, crossbow archery and short golf. Voorthuizen is a small town close to the site, while Amersfoort, Apeldoorn and the Hoge Veluwe National Park are all easily visited by car. Just 1 km. away is Recreatieplas Zeumeren, a large lake with a sandy beach and wealth of facilities – ideal for a picnic or just a stroll around the lake.

Facilities: One clean, heated toilet block has free showers and some washbasins in cubicles. Good facilities for children and disabled visitors. Some private sanitary facilities to rent on pitches. Shop. Restaurant, bar, snack bar. Large swimming complex. Sauna and Turkish steam bath. Large adventure play area for children. Pony riding and lessons. Minigolf. 10-pin bowling. Short golf. Tennis. Football. Basketball. Children's farm. Entertainment and children's club. Hairdresser. Bicycle hire. WiFi over part of site (charged). Off site: Walking and cycling in the National Park. Old cities of Apeldoorn and Amersfoort. Kröller-Müller Museum (one of the world's largest collections of Van Gogh paintings).

Open: 23 March - 27 October.

Directions: Approaching on A1 motorway, take exit 16 and drive to Voorthuizen. In Voorthuizen at first roundabout turn right and drive through the village. Then take first turn right (Bosweg). At the end turn left to the site entrance on the right (500 m).

GPS: 52.187556, 5.630976

Charges guide

Per unit incl. 2 persons and electricity	€ 22,00 - € 35,00
private sanitary facilities	€ 8,00 - € 10,00
extra person	€ 5,00

No credit cards.

You might like to know

The kids' club (3-10 years) provides hours of fun with crafts, games and theatre, and features the loveable characters, Keessie and Willie.

- ☑ Multi-lingual children's club – pre-school
- ☑ Multi-lingual children's club – 5-10 year olds
- ☑ Multi-lingual children's club – 10-14 year olds
- ☑ Creative crafts
- ☑ Bicycle hire for children
- ☑ Facilities for children in the wash blocks
- ☑ Children's pool
- ☑ Children's play area
- ○ Crèche and/or babysitting
- ☑ Local information of interest for children

Facilities: Eight modern sanitary units and a beautifully presented block for children. Private en-suite facilities to rent for eight touring pitches. Shop and bar (both open all year). Restaurant/takeaway (1/4-30/9). Swimming and paddling pools (heated 1/4-30/9) with water slide, sauna and solarium. Indoor play area for children. Bicycle hire. Tennis. Volleyball. Basketball. Terrace. Small animal park. WiFi (charged). Off site: Fishing 1 km. Riding 2 km. Golf 4 km. Running, cycling and walking tracks from site.

Open: All year.

Directions: Site is 60 km. east of Arnhem close to the border with Germany. From Winterswijk take N319 southeast for 2 km. then turn right onto De Slingeweg. Site is on outskirts of Winterswijk Brinkheurne.

GPS: 51.952137, 6.736899

Charges guide

Per unit incl. 2 persons and electricity € 19,00 - € 27,00	
extra person € 3,25	
dog € 3,00	

Recreatiepark Het Winkel

De Slingeweg 20, NL-7115 AG Winterswijk (Gelderland)
t: 0543 513025   e: info@hetwinkel.nl
alanrogers.com/NL6412   www.hetwinkel.com

Accommodation: ☑ Pitch   ☑ Mobile home/chalet   ○ Hotel/B&B   ☑ Apartment

Recreatiepark Het Winkel is a friendly family campsite in the middle of unspoilt countryside, surrounded by woodland in the Achterhoek region. The generous pitches (300 for touring) are serviced with electricity, water and drain. Some meadow areas (without electricity) are only used for tents. Eight chalets are available to rent. There are large open spaces for leisure and sporting activities and a wide range of facilities for all the family. Cycling, running and walking routes start from the site. The Achterhoek region has the most extensive network of cycle paths in the Netherlands. The site provides a wide variety of sporting opportunities and in the high season there is an activity programme for children of all ages. There are many interesting places to visit nearby such as Erve Brookert which is a picturesque, historic building from 1875, originally a farmhouse, hayloft and klompenhuis where clogs were made, and now is open to the public, with a tea garden (limited opening).

You might like to know

There is daily entertainment for all. Children's facilities include the swimming pool, the mega indoor playground, many games and sports. For the little ones there are stories in the flower garden.

☑ Multi-lingual children's club – pre-school
☑ Multi-lingual children's club – 5-10 year olds
☑ Multi-lingual children's club – 10-14 year olds
☑ Creative crafts
☑ Bicycle hire for children
☑ Facilities for children in the wash blocks
☑ Children's pool
☑ Children's play area
○ Crèche and/or babysitting
☑ Local information of interest for children

Facilities:
Facilities: Four heated toilet blocks include bathrooms for children and a fully equipped launderette. Well stocked supermarket, bar, restaurant and takeaway (all open all season). Games and TV rooms. Indoor and outdoor swimming pools (not guarded). Tennis. Minigolf. Pétanque. Adventure play areas. Bicycle hire. Small BMX track. Outdoor chess. Riding. Fishing. Children's club and evening entertainment. WiFi throughout (charged). Max. 2 dogs per pitch. Off site: Golf 2 km.

Open: 28 March - 2 November.

Directions: From the A67 between Eindhoven and Venlo take exit 38 (direction Helden). At lights turn right to Koningslust and after 2 km. turn right again to site following camping signs.

GPS: 51.34897, 5.96101

Charges guide

Per unit incl. 2 persons and electricity (plus meter)	€ 31,75
extra person	€ 5,00
dog	€ 4,85

No credit cards.

Netherlands – Panningen

Camping & Speelparadijs Beringerzand

Heide 5, NL-5981 NX Panningen (Limburg)
t: 0773 072 095 e: info@beringerzand.nl
alanrogers.com/NL6525 www.beringerzand.nl

Accommodation: ☑ Pitch ☑ Mobile home/chalet ○ Hotel/B&B ○ Apartment

The history of this friendly site dates back more than 100 years to when it was established as a holiday resort for members of the Lazarist religious congregation. The park and its historic building (now the Patershof restaurant) have, for the last 40 years, been developed as a holiday paradise for young families. Beringerzand is set amongst the lovely villages and small lakes of the wooded area between the De Peel Natural Park and the Muse river. The 21-hectare site offers 375 spacious touring pitches, all with electricity (10A), TV, water and waste water, arranged around the edges of green fields. There are currently also 140 privately owned chalets. The fields have been very well designed and include various activity areas appropriate to different age groups. Very good amenities provide activities in both good and bad weather with indoor and outdoor pools, an indoor play centre and a variety of sports. Children's clubs are organised, as is evening entertainment. The Patershof restaurant is special, with good value meals and room for children to play and read books.

You might like to know

The site offers four special camping areas according to age: 'Mischief' for families with children under 8, 'Exciting' for under 10s, 'Adventurous' for under 13s, 'Enjoyment' for all ages and small-scale camping.

- ☑ Multi-lingual children's club – pre-school
- ☑ Multi-lingual children's club – 5-10 year olds
- ☑ Multi-lingual children's club – 10-14 year olds
- ☑ Creative crafts
- ☑ Bicycle hire for children
- ☑ Facilities for children in the wash blocks
- ☑ Children's pool
- ☑ Children's play area
- ○ Crèche and/or babysitting
- ☑ Local information of interest for children

Facilities: Five main toilet blocks, four heated by solar panels, provide toilets, washbasins (open and in cubicles) and showers. Washbasins for children. Heated baby rooms with changing mat and bath. Facilities for disabled visitors in one block. Laundry. Motorcaravan services. Supermarket, restaurant, bar, snack bar and swimming pools (all open as site). Entertainment and activities. Watersports, climbing wall and minigolf. Bicycle and go-cart hire. Tennis. Dogs are not accepted. WiFi over site (charged). Off site: Riding 2 km. Golf 7 km.

Open: 4 April - 2 November.

Directions: From Utrecht follow the A2 south towards Eindhoven, then Maastricht. Take exit for Antwerpen and follow signs for Eersel. From Eersel follow site signs.

GPS: 51.33623, 5.29373

Charges guide

Per unit incl. 2 persons
and electricity € 23,50 - € 56,50

Netherlands – Eersel

Recreatiepark TerSpegelt

Postelseweg 88, NL-5521 RD Eersel (Noord-Brabant)
t: 0497 512 016 e: info@terspegelt.nl
alanrogers.com/NL6630 www.terspegelt.nl

Accommodation: ☑ Pitch ☑ Mobile home/chalet ○ Hotel/B&B ○ Apartment

Camping TerSpegelt is a large, attractively laid out site set around three (unsupervised) lakes used for sports, non-motorised boating, swimming and fishing. The site has 855 pitches, with 481 for touring units and tents, and 70 cabins, chalets and mobile homes for rent, plus various types of tent. All touring pitches have electricity (6/16A Europlug), and 347 also have water and drainage, and some have lakeside views. We can recommend this site to families with children (pushchairs useful) and people who like to participate in organised activities (sports and outdoor activities, campfires and themed dinners). Starbeach is a covered playground with a beautiful in-house beach and spectacular play equipment such as an eight metre high castle – ideal for playing and swimming if the weather is poor. There is a 120 m. aerial runway. You can enjoy an evening meal at the beachside restaurant, De Wijde Blick, and relax with a drink in the bar, along with plenty of evening entertainment.

You might like to know

For something quite different, why not try a water dome tent? This is a fully equipped tent on a wooden raft, complete with 4 beds, a small stove, a brazier, barbecue area and a hammock for relaxing.

○ Multi-lingual children's club – pre-school
☑ Multi-lingual children's club – 5-10 year olds
☑ Multi-lingual children's club – 10-14 year olds
☑ Creative crafts
○ Bicycle hire for children
☑ Facilities for children in the wash blocks
○ Children's pool
☑ Children's play area
○ Crèche and/or babysitting
☑ Local information of interest for children

Facilities:
Four sanitary blocks have showers, washbasins, both open and in cabins, a bathroom and a baby bath. Washing machine and dryer. Motorcaravan services. Supermarket, restaurant/bar and snack bar (18/4-28/9). Heated indoor (5/4-28/9) and outdoor (26/4-31/8) swimming pools. Disco. Recreation room. Football. Tennis. Nine hole golf course, school and driving range. Bicycle hire. Watersports. Play areas (including indoor). Animal corner. Internet access and WiFi throughout (charged). Organised activities in July/Aug. Max. 2 dogs. Off site: Opposite the site is a brand new 9-hole golf course. Fishing 3 km. Riding 15 km. Golf 20 km.

Open: 4 April - 26 October.

Directions: Travelling east or west on the N284 Eindhoven-Reusel Road turn south at second traffic lights in Bladel and follow camping signs to site.

GPS: 51.34406, 5.226939

Charges guide

Per unit incl. 2 persons and electricity € 23,00 - € 36,00	
with own sanitary unit € 31,00 - € 49,00	
extra person € 2,00 - € 4,00	
dog (max. 2) € 5,00	

Netherlands – Bladel

Recreatiepark De Achterste Hoef

Troprijt 10, NL-5531 NA Bladel (Noord-Brabant)
t: 0497 381 579   e: info@achterstehoef.nl
alanrogers.com/NL6710   www.achterstehoef.nl/nl/index_en.lp

Accommodation: ☑ Pitch ☑ Mobile home/chalet ○ Hotel/B&B ○ Apartment

This quite large campsite is to be found off the N284 at Bladel in Noord-Brabant. It is an ideal location for cycling and walking and is close to the Belgian border. A family-oriented site, it offers good quality facilities which are well maintained and kept very clean. There are 390 touring pitches, all fully serviced and 22 with their own sanitation, sited near the lake. The touring pitches are 80-150 sq.m. in size with many amongst the trees, but some are on open meadows and some divided by young shrubs. There are also seasonal and static caravan places, but these are kept apart and mostly in one area. On entering the site you find all the main service buildings alongside reception. Opposite reception is an interestingly landscaped minigolf. To the rear of the site is a lake and beach area, with a dedicated section for swimming. Since being highly commended for families in 2012, the site has added a nine-hole golf course, a driving range, a BMX track and a large, wooded and fenced area for dog walking.

You might like to know

De Achterste Hoef has extensive facilities, including a covered swimming pool, heated outdoor pool, swimming lake with water slide, play area with air trampoline, indoor play area, adventure minigolf, small train, theatre, disco and kids' club.

- ☑ Multi-lingual children's club – pre-school
- ☑ Multi-lingual children's club – 5-10 year olds
- ☑ Multi-lingual children's club – 10-14 year olds
- ☑ Creative crafts
- ☑ Bicycle hire for children
- ☑ Facilities for children in the wash blocks
- ☑ Children's pool
- ☑ Children's play area
- ○ Crèche and/or babysitting
- ☑ Local information of interest for children

Camping De Krabbeplaat

Oude Veerdam 4, NL-3231 NC Brielle (Zuid-Holland)
t: 0181 412 363 e: info@krabbeplaat.nl
alanrogers.com/NL6980 www.krabbeplaat.nl

Accommodation: ☑ Pitch ☑ Mobile home/chalet ○ Hotel/B&B ○ Apartment

Camping De Krabbeplaat is a family run site situated near the ferry port in a wooded, recreation area next to the Brielse Meer lake. There are 448 spacious pitches, with 68 for touring units, all with 10A electricity, cable connections and a water supply nearby. A nature conservation plan exists to ensure the site fits into its natural environment. The lake and its beaches provide the perfect spot for watersports and relaxation and the site has its own harbour where you can moor your own boat. This excellent site is very convenient for the Europort ferry terminal. Plenty of cultural opportunities can be found in the historic towns of the area. Because of the large range of amenities and the tranquil nature of the site, De Krabbeplaat is perfect for families and couples.

You might like to know

De Krabbeplaat is situated in beautiful surroundings next to the Brielse Meer lake, just a stone's throw from the sea, with unlimited things to do. Young or old, family or couple, everyone feels at home at De Krabbeplaat.

- ☑ Multi-lingual children's club – pre-school
- ☑ Multi-lingual children's club – 5-10 year olds
- ☑ Multi-lingual children's club – 10-14 year olds
- ☑ Creative crafts
- ○ Bicycle hire for children
- ☑ Facilities for children in the wash blocks
- ☑ Children's pool
- ☑ Children's play area
- ○ Crèche and/or babysitting
- ☑ Local information of interest for children

Facilities: One large and two smaller heated toilet blocks in traditional style provide separate toilets, showers and washing cabins. High standards of cleanliness. Dedicated unit for disabled campers and provision for babies. Warm water is free of charge. Dishwasher (free). Launderette. Motorcaravan services. Supermarket, snack bar, restaurant and takeaway (all season). Recreation room. Youth centre. Tennis. Playground and play field. Animal farm. Bicycle and children's pedal hire. Canoe, surf, pedal boat and boat hire. Fishing. WiFi over site (charged). Six cabins to rent. Off site: Golf 3 km. Riding 6 km. Beach 7 km.

Open: 28 March - 30 September.

Directions: From the Amsterdam direction take the A4 (Europoort), then the A15 (Europoort). Take exit for Brielle on N57 and, just before Brielle, site is signed.

GPS: 51.9097, 4.18536

Charges guide

Per unit incl. 2 persons and electricity	€ 18,00 - € 25,00
extra person	€ 3,30
child (under 12 yrs)	€ 2,80

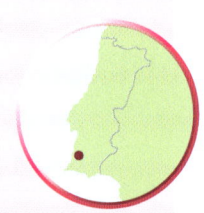

Facilities: Eight toilet blocks provide comprehensive facilities, including for children and disabled visitors. Large supermarket. Bar. Restaurant. Crêperie. Takeaway. Outdoor swimming pool (April-Oct). Covered pool and wellness centre (Feb-Dec). Sports field. Games room. Play area, farm and play house. Tennis. Bicycle hire. Activity and entertainment programme. Mobile homes and caravans for rent. Caravan repair and servicing. The site's own debit card system is used for payment at all facilities. WiFi around central complex (free), Off site: Vicentina coast and the Alentejo Natural Park. Cycle and walking tracks. Fishing 6 km. Beach 7 km. Riding 10 km. Sailing and boat launching 12 km. Shops, bars and restaurants in Odemira 12 km. Resort of Vila Nova de Milfontes 20 km.

Open: All year (facilities all closed in January).

Directions: Odemira is on the Atlantic coast 75 km. north of Lagos at the southern tip. From the N120 (Odemira-Lagos), at roundabout 3 km. west of Odemira turn west on N393 towards Milfontes. In 6.5 km turn southwest on N393-1 towards Cabo Sardao and Zambujeira do Mar. Site is on the left in 1.6 km.

GPS: 37.60422, -8.73142

Charges guide

Per unit incl. 2 or 3 persons and electricity	€ 20,00 - € 37,50
extra person	€ 7,00 - € 10,00
child (6-12 yrs)	€ 5,00 - € 8,00
dog	€ 2,50 - € 8,00

Zmar-Eco Camping Resort

Herdade A de Mateus EN393/1, San Salvador, P-7630 Odemira (Beja)
t: 283 690 010   e: info@zmar.eu
alanrogers.com/PO8175   www.zmar.eu

Accommodation: ☑ Pitch ☑ Mobile home/chalet ○ Hotel/B&B ○ Apartment

Zmar is an exciting project which was set up in 2009. The site is located near Zambujeira do Mar, on the Alentejo coast. It is a highly ambitious initiative developed along very strict environmental lines. Renewable resources such as locally harvested timber and recycled plastic are used wherever possible and the main complex of buildings is clean-cut and impressive. A terrace overlooks an open-air pool that seems to go on for ever. The 288 pitches are 90 sq.m. and some, mainly for tents or smaller caravans and motorcaravans, benefit from artificial shade. Caravans and wood-clad mobile homes are also available for rent. In addition to the outdoor pool, the complex features an indoor pool area with a wave machine and a wellness centre. The very large and innovative play park for children has climbing nets, labyrinths and caves. There is also a children's farm and a large play house. For adults, many sporting amenities are available around the resort's 81-hectare park. Although several hundred olive trees were planted all over the site, many of these have sadly not survived and a new programme of planting is planned.

You might like to know

Zmar is a new concept in eco-tourism and many children's activities reflect these concerns.

- ○ Multi-lingual children's club – pre-school
- ☑ Multi-lingual children's club – 5-10 year olds
- ☑ Multi-lingual children's club – 10-14 year olds
- ☑ Creative crafts
- ☑ Bicycle hire for children
- ☑ Facilities for children in the wash blocks
- ☑ Children's pool
- ☑ Children's play area
- ☑ Crèche and/or babysitting
- ☑ Local information of interest for children

Turiscampo

EN125, Espiche, P-8600-109 Lagos (Faro)
t: 282 789 265 e: info@turiscampo.com
alanrogers.com/PO8202 www.yellohvillage.co.uk/camping/turiscampo

Accommodation: ☑ Pitch ☑ Mobile home/chalet ○ Hotel/B&B ○ Apartment

Turiscampo is an outstanding site which has been thoughtfully refurbished and updated since it was purchased by the friendly Coll family in 2003 and the transformation is on-going. The site provides 268 pitches for touring units, mainly in rows of terraces, all with 6/10A electricity and some with shade. There are 38 deluxe pitches with water and drain. The upper terraces are occupied by 132 bungalows for rent. Just down the road is the fashionable resort of Praia de Luz, with its beach, shops, bars and restaurants. Head west and the road takes you to Sagres and the wild western tip of the Algarve. Portugal's 'Land's End' has remained unspoiled and there are numerous rocky coves and little sandy beaches to explore. The headland at Cabo de Sao Vicente, has a working lighthouse and is well worth a visit, especially at sunset. Head east and you will come to the pleasant town of Lagos and beyond that, the whole of the Algarve with its beaches, little villages, fashionable resorts and bustling cities. This is a very good site for families, with wonderful facilities for children and plenty of activities in high season.

You might like to know

Children can learn the basics of Tai Chi with our fully qualified instructors.

○ Multi-lingual children's club – pre-school
☑ Multi-lingual children's club – 5-10 year olds
☑ Multi-lingual children's club – 10-14 year olds
☑ Creative crafts
○ Bicycle hire for children
☑ Facilities for children in the wash blocks
☑ Children's pool
☑ Children's play area
○ Crèche and/or babysitting
☑ Local information of interest for children

Facilities: Two toilet blocks provide outstanding facilities. There is a third facility beneath the pool. Spacious controllable showers. Hot water throughout. Delightful children and baby room. Facilities for disabled visitors. Dog shower. Laundry facilities. Shop. Gas supplies. Modern restaurant/bar with buffet and mexican-style meals. Pizza bar and takeaway. Swimming pools (March-Sept) with extensive terrace and jacuzzi. Aquagym. Wellness facility. Bicycle hire. Entertainment on the bar terrace. Miniclub (5-12 yrs, 15/6-15/9). Two playgrounds. Boules. Archery. Multisports court. Cable TV. Internet and WiFi (partial coverage) on payment. Bungalows to rent. Off site: Bus to Lagos and other towns from gate. Praia da Luz village 1.5 km. Beach, watersports, sailing and fishing 2.5 km. Lagos 6 km. Riding 7 km.

Open: All year.

Directions: Site is 90 km west of Faro. From A22 Spain-Algarve motorway exit 1, follow N120 to Lagos then head west on N125, following signs for Luz. The impressive entrance is 3.8 km. on the right.

GPS: 37.10111, -8.73278

Charges guide

Per unit incl. 2 persons and electricity	€ 18,00 - € 35,00
extra person	€ 4,00 - € 7,00
child (3-10 yrs)	no charge - € 4,00
dog	€ 5,00

Facilities: Two attractive and well maintained log-built toilet blocks, both recently renovated. Facilities for disabled visitors. Laundry facilities. Motorcaravan services. Shop (March-Nov). Café serves light meals, snacks and drinks apparently with flexible closing hours. Play area. Bowling. Fishing. Bicycle hire. Canoe hire. Climbing walls. Communal barbecue. WiFi. Off site: Town within walking distance. Riding 5 km. Golf 15 km. Trilav National Park. Guided tours in the Soca valley and around Slovenia start from the campsite.

Open: All year.

Directions: Approaching Kobarid from Tolmin on 102, just before Kobarid turn right on 203 towards Bovec and after 100 m. take descending slip road to right and keep more or less straight on to Napoléon's bridge (about 500 m). Cross bridge and site is on left in 100 m.

GPS: 46.25075, 13.58658

Charges guide

Per unit incl. 2 persons and electricity	€ 25,00 - € 28,00
extra person	€ 10,50 - € 12,00
child (7-12 yrs)	€ 5,25 - € 6,00
dog	€ 2,00

Kamp Koren Kobarid

Ladra 1b, SLO-5222 Kobarid (Slovenia)
t: 053 891 311   e: info@kamp-koren.si
alanrogers.com/SV4270   www.kamp-koren.si

Accommodation: ☑ Pitch   ☑ Mobile home/chalet   ○ Hotel/B&B   ○ Apartment

Kamp Koren, Slovenia's first ecological site, is in a quiet location above the Soca river gorge, within easy walking distance of Kobarid. The site has 90 slightly sloping pitches, all with 6/16A electricity and ample tree shade. It is deservedly very popular with those interested in outdoor sports, be it on the water, in the mountains or in the air. At the same time, its peaceful situation makes it an ideal choice for those seeking a relaxing break. There are six well equipped chalets, and a shady area mainly for tents was opened in 2014 at the top of the site. Kobarid, probably best approached via Udine in Italy, is a pleasant country town, with easy access to nearby rivers, valleys and mountains, which alone justify a visit to Kamp Koren. But most British visitors will remember it for the opportunity it provides to fill that curious gap in their knowledge of European history. The local museum in Kobarid was recently voted European Museum of the Year and is excellent.

You might like to know

Why not explore the Triglav National Park in the Julian Alps, which features Slovenia's largest glacial lake, Lake Bohinj.

○ Multi-lingual children's club – pre-school
○ Multi-lingual children's club – 5-10 year olds
○ Multi-lingual children's club – 10-14 year olds
○ Creative crafts
☑ Bicycle hire for children
○ Facilities for children in the wash blocks
○ Children's pool
☑ Children's play area
☑ Crèche and/or babysitting
○ Local information of interest for children

Facilities: Four good, heated sanitary blocks with free hot water and facilities for babies and disabled visitors. Motorcaravan services. Laundry with washing machines and dryers. Kitchen with cooking rings, oven and microwave. Small shop at reception. Bar, restaurant and takeaway. Minigolf. Tennis. Fitness trail. Fishing. Canoe hire. Children's club. WiFi (free). Off site: Swimming pool complex adjacent to site (free for campers as is a visit to the zoo). Golf 11 km. Motor racing track at Ring Knutstorp 8 km.

Open: 17 April - 20 September.

Directions: From Malmö: drive towards Lund and follow road no. 108 to Röstånga. From Stockholm: turn off at Östra Ljungby and take road no. 13 to Röstånga. In Röstånga drive through the village on road no. 108 and follow the signs.

GPS: 55.996583, 13.28005

Charges guide

Per unit incl. 2 persons
and electricity € 25,00 - € 33,00

No credit cards.

Röstånga Camping & Bad

Blinkarpsvägen 3, S-268 68 Röstånga (Skåne Län)
t: 043 591 064 e: nystrand@msn.com
alanrogers.com/SW2630 www.rostangacamping.se

Accommodation: ☑ Pitch ☑ Mobile home/chalet ○ Hotel/B&B ○ Apartment

Beside the Söderåsen National Park, this scenic campsite has its own fishing lake and many activities for the whole family. There are 180 large, level, grassy pitches with electricity (10A) and a quiet area for tents with a view over the fishing lake. The tent area has its own service building and several barbecue places. A large holiday home and 21 pleasant cabins are available to rent all year round. A pool complex adjacent to the site provides a 50 m. swimming pool, three children's pools and a water slide, all heated during peak season. Activities are arranged on the site in high season, including a children's club with exciting activities such as treasure hunts and gold panning, and for adults, aquarobics, Nordic walking and tennis. The Söderåsen National Park offers hiking and bicycle trails. The friendly staff will be happy to help you to plan interesting excursions in the area.

You might like to know

When children are not busy at the Kids' Club, in the playgrounds and on the bouncy cushions, there is an exciting forest walk with a tyre swing, tunnels and a stream.

○ Multi-lingual children's club – pre-school
☑ Multi-lingual children's club – 5-10 year olds
○ Multi-lingual children's club – 10-14 year olds
☑ Creative crafts
○ Bicycle hire for children
☑ Facilities for children in the wash blocks
☑ Children's pool
☑ Children's play area
○ Crèche and/or babysitting
☑ Local information of interest for children

Facilities: Two heated sanitary buildings provide the usual facilities with showers on payment. Kitchen with good cooking facilities and sinks. Dining room. Laundry facilities. Units for disabled visitors. Motorcaravan services. Shop. Restaurant, takeaway and pub. Live music evenings. TV room. Outdoor swimming pool. Relaxation centre with sauna and jacuzzi (charged). Well equipped gym. Water slide (charged). WiFi (charged). Riding. Minigolf. Tennis. Boules. Playground. Clay pigeon shooting. Boat hire (canoe, rowing, motor, pedalo). Outside gym/fitness area. WiFi over site (charged). Off site: Shopping centre and golf 13 km. Havets hus (marine museum) 30 km. Nordens Ark (animal park) 40 km.

Open: All year.

Directions: From E6, north of Uddevalla, at Torpmotet exit take 161 road towards Lysekil. At Rotviksbro roundabout take 160 road towards Orust. Exit to site is located 2 km. further on left where four flags fly. Follow signs for 4 km. along one-way road for motorcaravans and caravans.

GPS: 58.31478, 11.72344

Charges guide

Per pitch incl. electricity	SEK 230 - 450
extra person	SEK 100

Hafsten SweCamp Resort

Hafsten 120, S-451 96 Uddevalla (Västra Götalands Län)
t: 052 264 4117 e: info@hafsten.se
alanrogers.com/SW2725 www.hafsten.se

Accommodation: ☑ Pitch ☑ Mobile home/chalet ○ Hotel/B&B ○ Apartment

This privately owned site on the west coast is situated on a peninsula overlooking the magnificent coastline of Bohuslän. Open all year, it is a lovely, peaceful, terraced site with a beautiful, shallow and child friendly sandy beach and many nature trails in the vicinity. There are 220 touring pitches, all with electricity (10A), 115 of them with water and drainage. In all, there are 370 pitches including a tent area and 62 cabins of a high standard. There are plenty of activities available ranging from horse riding at the stables on the campsite's own farm to an 86 m. long water chute. Organised live music evenings with visiting performers are arranged during the summer. Almost any activity can be arranged on the site or elsewhere by the friendly owners if they are given advance notice. Amenities include two clean and well maintained service buildings, a pub, a fully licensed restaurant with wine from their own French vineyard, a well stocked shop and a takeaway. Reception is open and welcoming with natural light used to great effect, and where the new fitness and wellness facilities can be found.

You might like to know

This is a privately owned, peaceful site with plenty to keep the whole family occupied all year round.

○ Multi-lingual children's club – pre-school
○ Multi-lingual children's club – 5-10 year olds
○ Multi-lingual children's club – 10-14 year olds
○ Creative crafts
○ Bicycle hire for children
○ Facilities for children in the wash blocks
☑ Children's pool
☑ Children's play area
☑ Crèche and/or babysitting
○ Local information of interest for children

Facilities: Five toilet blocks of excellent quality with washbasin cubicles, showers, family rooms, a children's bathroom, sun beds, saunas and make up rooms. Wellness centre and hairdressers. Units for disabled visitors. Kitchen with cookers, microwaves, sinks and industrial grade dishwashers. Extensive laundry facilities. Motorcaravan services. Large supermarket. Fully licensed restaurant. Heated pool (peak season). Games and TV rooms. Themed minigolf. Bicycle hire. Children's club. Boat hire, excursions and seal safaris. Internet and WiFi. Conference room. B&B. DaftöLand adventure park. Off site: Ferry to Norway (Sandefjord) from Strömstad. The Koster islands (ferry from Strömstad). Golf on three courses at Strömstad. Riding 3 km. Aquarium at Tjärnö 6 km. Rock carvings at Tanum 25 km.

Open: All year excl. 23 December - 6 January.

Directions: Daftö is 5 km. south of Strömstad on road 176. It is signed.

GPS: 58.904267, 11.200117

Charges guide

Per unit incl. electricity
and water SEK 200 - 470

Daftö Resort

S-452 97 Strömstad (Västra Götalands Län)
t: 052 626 040   e: info@dafto.se
alanrogers.com/SW2735   www.dafto.se

Accommodation: ☑ Pitch   ☑ Mobile home/chalet   ○ Hotel/B&B   ○ Apartment

This extremely high quality, family campsite, with a strong pirate theme, is beautifully situated on the west coast, 5 km. south of Strömstad. A very large site, terraced in parts, has both shady and open areas. In total there are 650 pitches with 310 for touring, all with electrical hook-ups (10A, CEE plugs). In addition, there are 130 modern, very well equipped cabins of various sizes and styles. Daftö Resort, with its DaftöLand adventure park (concessions for campers), has activities for all including boating, beach volleyball, walks and yoga, and all manner of theme-based activities for children including theatre, competitions and treasure hunting. Footpaths take you into the forest where not only mushrooms and blueberries, but deer and elk can be found. Bicycles and boats can be rented on site and boat trips and seal safaris are arranged. The facilities are of very high quality with everything you could possibly want in four clean and attractive blocks. The site supermarket has fresh food, bread, groceries and a range of other goods and toys. In peak season, the welcoming and fully licensed restaurant has a comprehensive menu for all ages.

You might like to know

In the exciting pirate aqua park, children will have a wonderful time and will want to stay for hours. Fortunately, the restaurant is very close.

○ Multi-lingual children's club – pre-school
☑ Multi-lingual children's club – 5-10 year olds
☑ Multi-lingual children's club – 10-14 year olds
☑ Creative crafts
○ Bicycle hire for children
☑ Facilities for children in the wash blocks
☑ Children's pool
☑ Children's play area
○ Crèche and/or babysitting
☑ Local information of interest for children

Facilities: Three sanitary blocks (two heated) provide a good supply of showers, washbasins and toilets. Baby rooms and facilities for disabled visitors. Good kitchen with cookers, microwaves and sinks. Hot water is free throughout. Well equipped laundry rooms. Sauna. Motorcaravan services. Well stocked shop (1/5-15/9). Snack bar. Adjacent licensed restaurant and bar. Takeaway. Playground. Bouncy castle. Water slide. Family entertainment and children's activities (high season). Minigolf. Sea fishing. WiFi. Chalets for rent.
Off site: Riding 2 km. Kolmården Zoo 4 km. Golf 18 km. The Göta Canal 30 km.

Open: All year.

Directions: From the E4 motorway take Kolmården exit (no. 126) 23 km. north of Norrköping. Follow signs for Kolmården and site is well signed.

GPS: 58.65972, 16.40065

Charges guide

Per pitch SEK 145 - 195	
electricity SEK 45	

First Camp Kolmården

S-618 34 Kolmården (Östergötlands Län)
t: 011 398 250   e: kolmarden@firstcamp.se
alanrogers.com/SW2805   www.firstcamp.se

Accommodation: ☑ Pitch ☑ Mobile home/chalet ◯ Hotel/B&B ◯ Apartment

This is a family site, located on Bråviken Bay on the Baltic coast 160 km. south of Stockholm. Open all year, the site is just 4 km. from Kolmården Zoo, one of Sweden's most popular family attractions. There are 300 pitches, of which 180 have electrical connections (10A). Some pitches have sea views; there is also a large beautiful wooded area for tents and 99 cabins of various standards for rent. A good range of amenities includes a 120 m. water slide and a children's playground. Adjacent to the site is a handicraft village and the Sjöstugans restaurant. With direct access to Bråviken Bay, it is possible to swim on site and there is a shallow, child friendly area. Fishing, notably for Baltic herring, is also popular.

You might like to know

There's a mini disco every Friday with karaoke for the kids. Screenings of famous films are interspersed with other children's club activities, such as barbecues and mini-Olympics.

- ☑ Multi-lingual children's club – pre-school
- ☑ Multi-lingual children's club – 5-10 year olds
- ☑ Multi-lingual children's club – 10-14 year olds
- ☑ Creative crafts
- ◯ Bicycle hire for children
- ☑ Facilities for children in the wash blocks
- ◯ Children's pool
- ◯ Children's play area
- ◯ Crèche and/or babysitting
- ☑ Local information of interest for children

Facilities: Five modern toilet blocks provide showers, two family bathrooms, baby bath, laundry facilities and provision for disabled visitors. Well stocked supermarket with bread (from late May). Hire shop. Bars (with TV), restaurant, café and takeaway. Entertainment (every night in season). Pool complex with heated outdoor pool, paddling pool, sunbathing decks, solarium, sauna and massage chair. Health and beauty salon. Fun park, adventure playground, Kiddies Club. Amusement arcade and bowling alley. Teenagers' room. Par 3 golf course. 18-hole pitch and putt. Bicycle hire. Coarse fishing with three lakes. WiFi (free). Off site: Bus stop 200 yds. Riding within 2 miles. Bicycle hire and boat launching 4 miles.

Open: 10-24 April, 18 May - 13 September.

Directions: From A3075 approach to Newquay-Perranporth road, turn towards Cubert and Holywell Bay. Continue through Cubert to park on the right.

GPS: 50.384983, -5.128933

Charges guide

Per unit incl. 2 persons and electricity £ 20.09 - £ 32.97	
extra person £ 6.27 - £ 11.96	
child (3-14 yrs) £ 1.73 - £ 8.68	
dog £ 4.60 - £ 5.90	

Families and couples only.
Many special discounts.

Trevornick Holiday Park

Holywell Bay, Newquay TR8 5PW (Cornwall)
t: 01637 830531 e: bookings@trevornick.co.uk
alanrogers.com/UK0220 www.trevornick.co.uk

Accommodation: ☑ Pitch ○ Mobile home/chalet ○ Hotel/B&B ○ Apartment

Trevornick, once a working farm, is a busy and well run family touring park providing a very wide range of amenities, close to one of Cornwall's finest beaches. A modern reception with welcoming staff sets the tone for your holiday. The park is well managed with facilities and standards constantly monitored. It has grown to provide pitches for caravanners and campers (no holiday caravans but 55 very well equipped Eurotents). There are 636 large grass pitches (600 with 16A electricity and 140 fully serviced) including TV connection, laid out on five level fields and two terraced areas. There are few trees but some good views. The recently refurbished farm buildings provide much entertainment, from bingo and quizzes to shows, discos and cabaret. Fishermen will enjoy the three lakes. The restaurant provides breakfast, lunch, dinner and takeaway food. There is an 18-hole golf course with a small, quiet club house offering bar meals; the views out to sea are wonderful. Next door is the Holywell Bay Fun Park (reduced rates) and the sandy beach is five minutes by car.

You might like to know

There is a brilliant sandy beach nearby.

- ☑ Multi-lingual children's club – pre-school
- ☑ Multi-lingual children's club – 5-10 year olds
- ☑ Multi-lingual children's club – 10-14 year olds
- ☑ Creative crafts
- ☑ Bicycle hire for children
- ☑ Facilities for children in the wash blocks
- ☑ Children's pool
- ☑ Children's play area
- ○ Crèche and/or babysitting
- ☑ Local information of interest for children

Facilities: Good toilet blocks adjacent to the pitches, well maintained and heated, include roomy showers, some with washbasins en suite. Baths on payment. Unit for disabled visitors. Facilities for babies. Laundry. Gas supplies. Motorcaravan services. Large general shop, restaurant, bars and takeaway (all 27/3-31/10). Heated swimming pools, outdoor 1/5-13/9, indoor all year. Fitness centre. Tennis. Crazy golf. Playground. Nature trail. Amusement centre with pool, table tennis and amusement machines. Children's room. Soft play area. WiFi over site (charged). Dogs are not accepted.
Off site: Regular minibus service to Paignton (timetable at reception) and public services from outside the park. Fishing, bicycle hire, riding and golf all within 2 miles.

Open: All year.

Directions: Park is south of Paignton in Goodrington Road between A379 coast road and B3203 ring road and is well signed on both.
GPS: 50.413533, -3.568667

Charges guide

Per unit incl. 2 persons and electricity	£ 18.15 - £ 35.50
tent pitch incl. 2 persons	£ 14.35 - £ 33.00
extra person	£ 5.00
child (4-14 yrs)	£ 4.00

Max. 6 persons per reservation.

Beverley Holidays

Goodrington Road, Paignton TQ4 7JE (Devon)
t: 01803 661978 e: info@beverley-holidays.co.uk
alanrogers.com/UK0870 www.beverley-holidays.co.uk

Accommodation: ☑ Pitch ☑ Mobile home/chalet ○ Hotel/B&B ○ Apartment

Beverley Park is an amazing holiday centre catering for every need. It has been developed and run by the Jeavons family for over 50 years to very high standards. It is popular, busy and attractively landscaped with marvellous views over Torbay. The pools, a cabaret area, bars and entertainment, are all run in an efficient and orderly manner. The park has 190 caravan holiday homes and 21 lodges, mainly around the central complex. There are 159 touring pitches in the lower areas of the park, all reasonably sheltered, some with views across the bay and some on slightly sloping ground. All pitches can take awnings and 87 have 16A electricity (15 m. cable), 42 have hardstanding and are fully serviced. Tents are accepted and a limited number of tent pitches have electrical connections. The park is open all year and reservations are essential for caravans in high season. Entertainment is organised at Easter and from early May in the Starlight Cabaret bar. There are indoor and outdoor pools, each one heated and supervised. The Oasis fitness centre provides a steam room, jacuzzi and an excellent fitness room. A member of the Best of British group.

You might like to know

Children will be kept busy with the Fantasy Island indoor soft play area, arts and crafts activities, face painting and pottery in Sandy's Shack.

○ Multi-lingual children's club – pre-school
☑ Multi-lingual children's club – 5-10 year olds
☑ Multi-lingual children's club – 10-14 year olds
☑ Creative crafts
○ Bicycle hire for children
☑ Facilities for children in the wash blocks
☑ Children's pool
☑ Children's play area
○ Crèche and/or babysitting
☑ Local information of interest for children

Facilities:
Two toilet blocks include family bathrooms and saunas. Laundry facilities. Motorcaravan services. Shop. Takeaway. Club, bars, restaurant. Entertainment for adults and children, day and evening. Outdoor pool with flume and terrace, and splash pad water play area (19/5-14/9). Indoor pool, sauna, paddling pool and fountain. Ten pin bowling. Climbing wall. Adventure golf. Games rooms. Good adventure play area. Indoor soft play area. WiFi in bars and cafés (free). Off site: Beach and golf 1 mile. Fishing and riding 2 miles. Bicycle hire and sailing 6 miles.

Open: 20 March - 2 November.

Directions: From Barnstaple take the A361 towards Ilfracombe and through Braunton. Turn left at Mullacott Cross roundabout towards Woolacombe and then right towards Mortehoe. Park is on the left before the village.

GPS: 51.184683, -4.1977

Charges guide

Per unit incl. up to 8 persons
and electricity £ 18.00 - £ 68.00

United Kingdom – Woolacombe

Twitchen House Holiday Park

Mortehoe Station Road, Woolacombe EX34 7ES (Devon)
t: 0844 7700 363 e: goodtimes@woolacombe.com
alanrogers.com/UK0730 www.woolacombe.co.uk

Accommodation: ☑ Pitch ☑ Mobile home/chalet ○ Hotel/B&B ○ Apartment

Set in the landscaped grounds of an attractive Edwardian country house, Twitchen House Holiday Park is owned by Woolacombe Bay Holiday Parks. Its most recent additions include a £2.5 million, state-of-the-art family entertainment centre featuring attractions such as a 10-pin bowling alley, a 3D cinema, an innovative craft centre and an exciting new indoor soft play area. The new Show Lounge provides a venue for daytime fun and varied evening entertainment, and a poolside terrace with coastal themed café and retro milkshake bar. Of the 600 pitches, 367 are for touring, 228 with 16A electricity, 120 on hardstanding, mostly arranged around oval access roads in hedged areas. The superb amenities include a pool complex that incorporates indoor and outdoor heated pools where lessons and other fun activities are organised. Twitchen House is very popular for families with children. There are excellent beaches nearby with a footpath down to the sea (20 minutes' walk). All the facilities of the three other Woolacombe Bay Holiday Villages are free to visitors.

You might like to know

Twitchen House is ideally located for exploring the coast, and is within walking distance of wide sandy bays, picture post-card villages, quaint fishing harbours and the rugged landscape of Exmoor. Discount vouchers for local attractions.

- ○ Multi-lingual children's club – pre-school
- ○ Multi-lingual children's club – 5-10 year olds
- ○ Multi-lingual children's club – 10-14 year olds
- ☑ Creative crafts
- ○ Bicycle hire for children
- ☑ Facilities for children in the wash blocks
- ☑ Children's pool
- ☑ Children's play area
- ○ Crèche and/or babysitting
- ☑ Local information of interest for children

Facilities: Three modern, heated toilet blocks, include private bathrooms (coin-operated, 20p) and 16 family shower cubicles. En-suite facilities for disabled visitors. Two laundry rooms. Motorcaravan services. Freezer for ice packs. Baby facilities. The leisure park café provides good value meals and a takeaway service for campers. Café opening hours and camping shop (with gas and basic food supplies) vary according to season and demand. TV and games room. WiFi throughout (charged). Dogs are accepted on the campsite but not in the leisure park (unstaffed day kennels available). Caravan storage. Off site: The charming town of Dartmouth and the South Hams beaches are nearby. Golf 0.5 miles. Riding 7 miles. Beach 6 miles. Fishing 9 miles.

Open: 28 March - 2 November.

Directions: From A38 at Buckfastleigh, take A384 to Totnes. Before the town centre turn right on A381 Kingsbridge road. After Halwell turn left at Totnes Cross garage, on A3122 to Dartmouth. Park is on right after 2.5 miles.

GPS: 50.357898, -3.675001

Charges guide

Per unit incl. 2 persons and electricity	£ 16.50 - £ 29.50
extra person over 2 yrs	£ 7.75
awning or extra small pup tent	£ 3.50
dog (contact site first)	£ 2.75

Free entry to leisure park for stays 2 nights or more.

Woodlands Grove Touring Park

Blackawton, Dartmouth, Totnes TQ9 7DQ (Devon)
t: 01803 712598 e: holiday@woodlandsgrove.com
alanrogers.com/UK0840 www.woodlands-caravanpark.com

Accommodation: ☑ Pitch ○ Mobile home/chalet ○ Hotel/B&B ○ Apartment

Woodlands is a pleasant surprise – from the road you have no idea of just what is hidden away deep in the Devon countryside. To achieve this, there has been sympathetic development of farm and woodland to provide a leisure park with a falconry centre and zoo park, which is open to the public and offers a range of activities and entertainment appealing to all ages. Taking 350 units, the camping and caravan site overlooks the woodland and the leisure park. The original, main field has been fully terraced to provide groups of four to eight flat, very spacious pitches with hedging, the majority hardstanding (90% have 10A electricity and a shared water tap, drain and rubbish bin). This field is used all season, with other fields brought into use during the busier months. The newest field has 120 pitches (with electricity) designed with a more open feel to provide space for larger groups or rallies. Children (and many energetic parents too!) will thoroughly enjoy a huge variety of imaginative adventure play equipment, amazing water coasters, toboggan runs, the new Sea Dragon Swing Ship, a white knuckle monster, the Avalanche, and much more.

You might like to know

Woodlands Grove is a previous winner of Alan Rogers Best Family Campsite. Free entry to Family Theme Park when you stay two nights or longer.

○ Multi-lingual children's club – pre-school
○ Multi-lingual children's club – 5-10 year olds
○ Multi-lingual children's club – 10-14 year olds
○ Creative crafts
○ Bicycle hire for children
☑ Facilities for children in the wash blocks
☑ Children's pool
☑ Children's play area
○ Crèche and/or babysitting
☑ Local information of interest for children

Facilities: Two modern fully tiled toilet blocks with underfloor heating. Roomy showers, family bathrooms and facilities for disabled visitors. Baby changing facilities. Two laundry rooms. Shop. Bar, restaurant and takeaway (2/6-1/9). Family entertainment (high season evenings). Two play areas. WiFi (free). Dog walk. Safari and medieval tents to rent. Access to Adventure Park – pay admission charges once, and receive free entry to the park for the following six days. Unique 'own a pony' experience on the Adventure park (booking required). Fishing. Off site: Greendale Farm shop. Woodbury Common and castle. Family pub within 2 miles. Exmouth and beaches 6 miles. Exeter 7 miles. Golf and riding 2 km.

Open: 15 March - 4 November.

Directions: From M5 exit 30 take A3052 signed Sidmouth, Seaton and Crealy. Keep straight on following Crealy signs. Site is on the right in under 2 miles. Using the A30/A303 from the east, join the M5 at exit 29 and travel south to exit 30, then as above.

GPS: 50.703606, -3.414967

Charges guide

Per unit incl. 2 persons and electricity	£ 25.00 - £ 37.50
extra person (2 yrs or over)	£ 7.00
dog	£ 3.00

Crealy Meadows Caravan Park

Sidmouth Road, Exeter EX5 1DR (Devon)
t: 01395 234888 e: stay@crealymeadows.co.uk
alanrogers.com/UK1125 www.crealymeadows.co.uk

Accommodation: ☑ Pitch ☑ Mobile home/chalet ○ Hotel/B&B ○ Apartment

Crealy Meadows is a new park in rural Devon developed by the owners of Crealy Adventure Park and situated adjacent to it. The multi-million pound investment has resulted in a well planned, purpose built park with excellent facilities. At present there are 99 serviced touring pitches (16A electricity, water and drainage) on neatly cut, level grass, and 21 hedged 'super' pitches (144 sq.m) with hardstanding. There are also pre-sited lodge tents in superbly themed safari camp or medieval village settings. These are really rather special and very well equipped with woodburning stoves and sinks. The Safari tents even boast a sleeping cupboard. Don't be surprised to see a knight of King Arthur's court guarding Camelot village, or a lioness and her cubs on watch beside the safari tents. There is direct gated access to the adventure park by means of pass cards, which saves queueing at the main entrance. Exmouth with its sandy beaches is about five miles away.

You might like to know

With Crealy Great Adventure Park as your back garden, you'll be able to pop in and out as often as you want. Ride the Maximus Rollercoaster, take to the air on The Flying Dutchman or make a splash on the Tidal Wave log flume.

○ Multi-lingual children's club – pre-school
○ Multi-lingual children's club – 5-10 year olds
○ Multi-lingual children's club – 10-14 year olds
☑ Creative crafts
○ Bicycle hire for children
☑ Facilities for children in the wash blocks
○ Children's pool
☑ Children's play area
○ Crèche and/or babysitting
☑ Local information of interest for children

Freshwater Beach Holiday Park

Burton Bradstock, Bridport DT6 4PT (Dorset)
t: 01308 897317 e: office@freshwaterbeach.co.uk
alanrogers.com/UK1780 www.freshwaterbeach.co.uk

Accommodation: ☑ Pitch ☑ Mobile home/chalet ○ Hotel/B&B ○ Apartment

Facilities: Three fully equipped toilet blocks – good provision for a busy beach park. Facilities for disabled visitors (Radar key). Baby care room (key system). Launderette. Bars with wide variety of entertainment and evening shows. Café. Good value supermarket and takeaway. Leisure complex with indoor pool, water play area for young children, gym and 10-pin bowling (family tickets available). Heated, supervised outdoor swimming and paddling pools (24/5-1/9). Activities for children. Two play areas. WiFi (charged). Off site: Bus stop on main road. Golf course 0.5 miles. Fishing possible from Chesil Bank. Abbotsbury Subtropical Gardens and Swannery 8 miles.

Open: 15 March - 9 November.

Directions: Park is immediately west of the village of Burton Bradstock, on the Weymouth-Bridport coast road (B3157).

GPS: 50.70500, -2.73867

Charges guide

Per unit incl. up to 6 persons
and electricity £ 16.00 - £ 42.00

car or boat £ 2.00

dog (max. 3) £ 2.50

Family run parks for families with direct access to their own private beach are rare in Britain and this one has the added advantage of being in beautiful coastal countryside in West Dorset. It now offers the Jurassic Fun Centre with pools, gym, bowling and a café. This building has a living, 'green' roof supporting native species of salt-tolerant grass and wildflowers which helps the complex merge into the landscape, and includes many eco-friendly features. The park is next to the sea and a beach of fine pebbles, sheltered from the wind by pebble banks. Approached by a fairly steep access road, the park itself is on level, open ground. The 500 touring pitches, 400 with 10A electricity, are on an open, undulating grass field connected by tarmac or hardcore roads. Caravan pitches are marked and evenly spaced in lines. Some tent pitches are in the main field, with others well spaced on a terraced field. There are 260 caravan holiday homes, with 60 for hire in a separate area. This lively holiday park has an extensive range of facilities, including an outdoor pool, a good value, licensed restaurant and main bar with evening entertainment in season.

You might like to know

Freshwater has a private beach and is surrounded by coastal and country footpaths. There are indoor pools, 10 pin bowling, a gym, seasonal entertainment and a children's club.

○ Multi-lingual children's club – pre-school
○ Multi-lingual children's club – 5-10 year olds
○ Multi-lingual children's club – 10-14 year olds
○ Creative crafts
○ Bicycle hire for children
☑ Facilities for children in the wash blocks
☑ Children's pool
☑ Children's play area
○ Crèche and/or babysitting
☑ Local information of interest for children

Facilities: Three toilet blocks have underfloor heating and washbasins in cubicles. Prefabricated units with hot water for the tent field. Toilets for disabled visitors and baby facilities. Excellent central launderette. Motorcaravan services. Entertainment and activity programme (high season). Outdoor pool (25/5-1/9). Indoor pool (66x30 ft). Well equipped gym, jacuzzi, steam room, sauna and hair and beauty suite. Games room. Adventure playground and play areas including indoor soft play area. Tents for rent. River fishing (permit). Bicycle hire. Archery. Dogs only allowed on certain fields. Off site: Riding stables. Golf 6 miles. Beach 20 miles. Dry ski slope 20 km.

Open: All year.

Directions: Park is well signed 1.5 miles east of Fordingbridge on the B3078.

GPS: 50.930267, -1.7602

Charges guide

Per unit incl. 2 persons and electricity	£ 10.00 - £ 60.00
extra person no charge	- £ 5.00
child no charge	
dog no charge	- £ 5.00

United Kingdom – Fordingbridge

Sandy Balls Holiday Village

Godshill, Fordingbridge SP6 2JZ (Hampshire)
t: 0845 270 2248   e: post@sandyballs.co.uk
alanrogers.com/UK2290   www.sandyballs.co.uk

Accommodation: ☑ Pitch   ☑ Mobile home/chalet   ○ Hotel/B&B   ○ Apartment

Sandy Balls sits high above the sweep of the Avon river near Fordingbridge, amidst woodland which is protected as a nature reserve. It has been in these guides for over 30 years and the entertainment facilities have been improved and developed. Very well run and open all year, the 120-acre park has many private holiday homes as well as 220 lodges for rent. In August, there is an additional unmarked area for 200 tents. The touring areas have 240 marked, hedged, serviced pitches for caravans and tents on part-hardstanding and part-grass, with 10/16A electricity and TV connections. A woodland leisure trail allows wild animals and birds to be observed in their natural surroundings and the attractions of the New Forest are close at hand. The heart of this holiday centre is the architecturally designed, multi-million pound 'village'. Within its traffic-free piazza are a bistro, pub, guest services bureau, gift shop, cycle shop, small supermarket and leisure club, all designed to blend in with the forest surroundings and provide space to relax and meet friends. A member of the Best of British group.

You might like to know

Don't forget to take your bike – it's a fun way to explore the New Forest National Park.

○ Multi-lingual children's club – pre-school
☑ Multi-lingual children's club – 5-10 year olds
☑ Multi-lingual children's club – 10-14 year olds
☑ Creative crafts
☑ Bicycle hire for children
☑ Facilities for children in the wash blocks
☑ Children's pool
☑ Children's play area
○ Crèche and/or babysitting
☑ Local information of interest for children

Facilities: Three toilet blocks include facilities for disabled visitors, a baby room and laundry facilities. Gas. Well stocked shop, bar, restaurant and takeaway (all season). Indoor leisure centre with pool, gym, etc. with trained staff (membership on either daily or weekly basis). Outdoor heated pool (25/5-5/9). Adventure play area. Tennis. Fishing. Bicycle hire. Entertainment programme. Special environmental Acorn activities for the family. WiFi (charged). Torches useful. Off site: The Norfolk coast, Felbrigg Hall, the Walsingham Shrine and the Norfolk Broads National Park are nearby. Many bird and nature reserves.

Open: 10 February - 2 January.

Directions: On A148 road from Holt to Cromer, after High Kelling, turn left just before Bodham village (international sign) signed Weybourne. Follow road for 1 mile to park.

GPS: 52.92880, 1.14953

Charges guide

Per unit incl. electricity	£ 18.65 - £ 33.85
with full services	£ 24.30 - £ 41.95
dog (max. 2)	£ 3.15 - £ 5.20
awning	£ 2.15 - £ 5.20

Min. 7 days in high season.
No single sex groups.

Kelling Heath Holiday Park

Weybourne, Holt, Sheringham NR25 7HW (Norfolk)
t: 01263 588181 e: info@kellingheath.co.uk
alanrogers.com/UK3430 www.kellingheath.co.uk

Accommodation: ☑ Pitch ☑ Mobile home/chalet ○ Hotel/B&B ○ Apartment

Not many parks can boast their own railway station and Kelling Heath's own halt on the North Norfolk Steam Railway gives access to the beach at Sheringham. Set in 250 acres of woodland and heathland, this very spacious holiday park offers freedom and relaxation with 300 large, level, grass touring pitches, all with 16A electricity and six are fully serviced. Together with 384 caravan holiday homes (36 to let, the rest privately owned), they blend easily into the part-wooded, part-open heath. A wide range of facilities provides activities for all ages. 'The Forge' has an entertainment bar and a family room, with comprehensive entertainment all season. The leisure centre provides an indoor pool, spa pool, sauna, steam rooms and gym. An adventure playground with assault course is nearby. The central reception area is attractively paved to provide a village square with an open-air bandstand. The park's natural environment allows for woodland walks, a nature trail and cycling trails, and a small lake for fishing (permit holders only). Other amenities include two hard tennis courts, an outdoor heated fun pool and play areas (some rather hidden from the pitches).

You might like to know

The Kelling Heath Holiday Park has its own Countryside Team and offers a range of nature activities such as evening bat walks.

○ Multi-lingual children's club – pre-school
☑ Multi-lingual children's club – 5-10 year olds
☑ Multi-lingual children's club – 10-14 year olds
○ Creative crafts
○ Bicycle hire for children
☑ Facilities for children in the wash blocks
☑ Children's pool
☑ Children's play area
○ Crèche and/or babysitting
○ Local information of interest for children

Brighouse Bay Holiday Park

Brighouse Bay, Borgue, Kirkcudbright DG6 4TS (Dumfries and Galloway)
t: 01557 870267 e: info@gillespie-leisure.co.uk
alanrogers.com/UK6950 www.brighouse-bay.co.uk

Accommodation: ☑ Pitch ☑ Mobile home/chalet ◯ Hotel/B&B ☑ Apartment

Hidden away within 1,200 exclusive acres, on a quiet, unspoilt peninsula, this spacious family park is only some 200 yards through bluebell woods from an open, sandy bay. It has exceptional all weather facilities, as well as golf and pony trekking. Over 90 percent of the 210 touring caravan pitches have 10/16A electricity, some with hardstanding and some with water, drainage and TV aerial. The three tent areas are on fairly flat, undulating ground and some pitches have electricity. There are 120 self-contained holiday caravans and lodges of which about 30 are let, the rest privately owned. On-site leisure facilities include a golf and leisure club with 16.5 m. pool, water features, jacuzzi, steam room, fitness room, games room (all on payment), golf driving range, bowling green and clubhouse bar and bistro. The 18-hole golf course extends onto the headland with superb views over the Irish Sea to the Isle of Man and Cumbria. A nine-hole family golf course is a popular attraction. Like the park, these facilities are open all year. This is a well run park with high standards.

You might like to know

Brighouse Bay has been developed along very eco-friendly principles, and is now one of the most environmentally sustainable campsites in the UK.

◯ Multi-lingual children's club – pre-school
◯ Multi-lingual children's club – 5-10 year olds
◯ Multi-lingual children's club – 10-14 year olds
◯ Creative crafts
☑ Bicycle hire for children
☑ Facilities for children in the wash blocks
◯ Children's pool
☑ Children's play area
◯ Crèche and/or babysitting
☑ Local information of interest for children

Facilities: The large, well maintained main toilet block includes 10 unisex cabins with shower, basin and WC, and 12 with washbasin and WC. A second, excellent block next to the tent areas has en-suite shower rooms (one for disabled visitors) and bathroom, separate washing cubicles, showers and baby room. Laundry facilities. Motorcaravan services. Gas supplies. Licensed shop. Bar, restaurant and takeaway (all year). Golf and Leisure Club with indoor pool (all year). Play area (incl. toddlers' area). Pony trekking. Quad bikes, boating pond, 10-pin bowling, playgrounds, putting. Nature trails. Coarse fishing ponds plus sea angling and an all-tide slipway for boating enthusiasts. Caravan storage. WiFi over site, free in bistro. Purpose built chalet for tourist information and leisure facility bookings. Off site: Small sandy beach nearby.

Open: All year.

Directions: In Kirkcudbright turn onto the A755 and cross river bridge. In 400 yds. turn left onto B727 at international camping sign. Or follow Brighouse Bay signs off A75 just east of Gatehouse of Fleet.

GPS: 54.7875, -4.1291

Charges guide

Per unit incl. 2 persons and electricity	£ 19.50 - £ 26.00
extra person	£ 3.00
child (5-15 yrs)	£ 2.00
dog	£ 2.00

Contact park for full charges.
Golf packages in low season.

Been to any good campsites lately?
We have

You'll find them here...

2015
the best campsites
in **Spain**
& Portugal
over 300 independent reviews

alan rogers

2015
the best campsites
in **Netherlands**
Belgium & Luxembourg
over 300 independent reviews

alan rogers

2015
the best campsites
in **Britain**
& Ireland
over 600 independent reviews

alan rogers

FREE
Travel Card

2015
the best campsites
in **Italy**
Croatia & Slovenia
over 300 independent reviews

alan rogers

2015
the best campsites
in **France**
over 1000 independent reviews

alan rogers

the **BIG**
selection
2015
over 1000 independent reviews

alan rogers

the best campsites
in **Europe**

FREE
Travel Card

The UK's market leading independent
guides to the best campsites

... also here...

101 great campsites, ideal for your specific hobby,
pastime or passion

Want independent campsite reviews at your fingertips?

You'll find them here...

Over 3,000 in-depth campsite reviews at
www.alanrogers.com

alan rogers

...and even here...

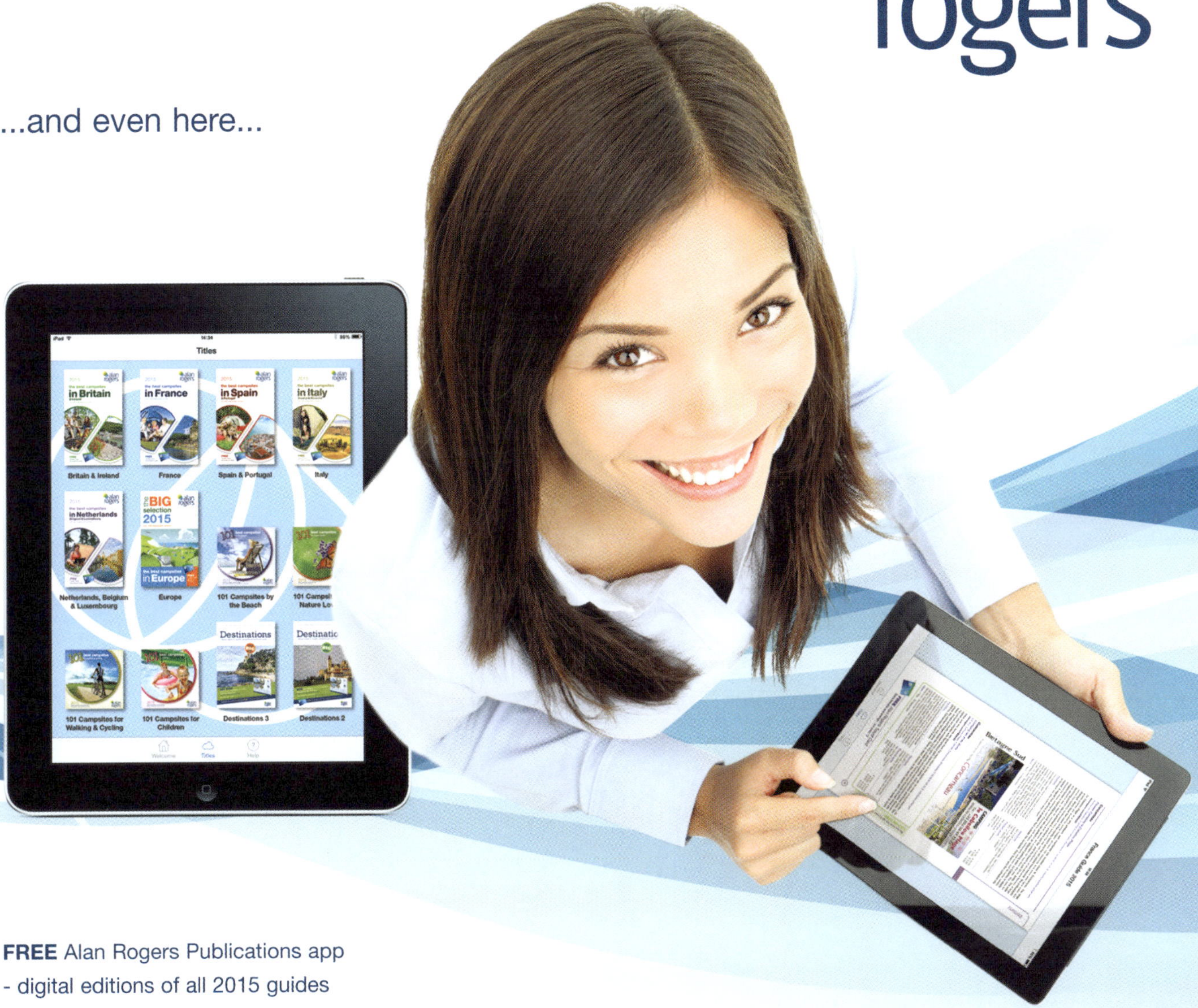

FREE Alan Rogers Publications app
- digital editions of all 2015 guides
alanrogers.com/digital

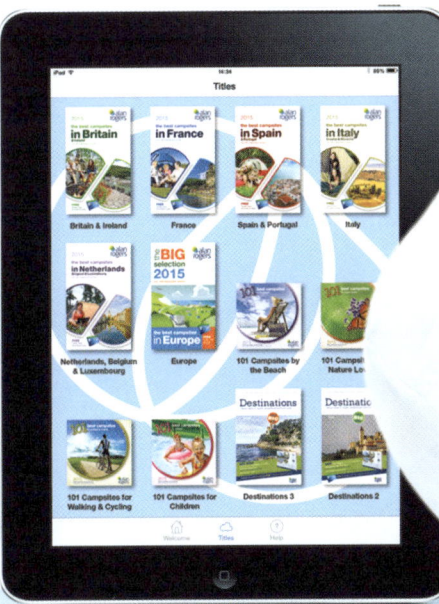

Want to book your holiday on one of Europe's top campsites?

We can do it for you. No problem.

The best campsites in the most popular regions - we'll take care of everything

alan rogers travel

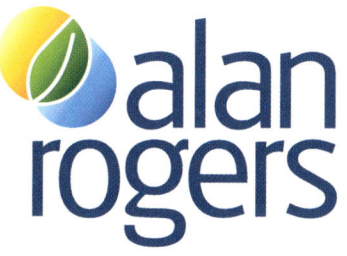

Discover the best campsites in Europe
with Alan Rogers

alanrogers.com
01580 214000

Index

Index

Index